THE COOKIE DOCTOR

THE COOKIE DOCTOR

An American Physician's Memoir of Life's Obstacles and Miracles

Peter T. Pugliese, MD

To order additional copies of this book, contact:
The Topical Agent LLC
7147 Bernville Road
Bernville, PA 19506
pattipugliese@outlook.com

610-488-1234
FAX 610-488-1818

www.petertpugliesemd.com

CONTENTS

DEDICATION

To all of those in the professions of healing,

To the patients whose lives we have held in our hands,

To the glory of God, for the gift of my own life,

And for the miracle of my wife and family.

FOREWORD

Nicholas Perricone, MD, FACN, CNS

For many years, I have had the honor and pleasure of being Dr. Peter Pugliese's friend and co-researcher. In our long discussions about philosophy and science, he has shared many of his experiences as a country doctor, which he has now compiled in this extraordinary book, *The Cookie Doctor*. When reading it, I learned more about the trials and tribulations he had faced on his way to becoming an outstanding physician and remarkable, innovative research scientist.

Beautifully written and intensely moving, *The Cookie Doctor* is a testament to the power of an unshakable faith. But this is not just a wonderful tale of inspiration and triumph over what seems almost insurmountable adversity at times, the kind of adversity that would have irreparably damaged a less courageous or dedicated person. In spite of the odds stacked against him, cruel twists of fate, and setback after setback, Dr. Pugliese persevered. He achieved and surpassed each of his goals, although not necessarily the goals he had originally pursued. His dream of a residency in Pathology—a dream previously guaranteed—was irrevocably stolen from him at the proverbial eleventh hour.

Pathology's loss—and it was a great loss as this brilliant researcher would have made discoveries and advances that we may never see—was the gain of the small Pennsylvania Dutch towns of Berks County. Here the bright, young doctor set up shop in the late 1950s, where many of The Cookie Doctor's experiences transpire. He became an integral and indispensable part of the community for over six decades.

The Cookie Doctor is a charming, entertaining, often comic, and at times, harrowing adventure story. Whether the Cookie Doctor is traveling on horseback through a raging blizzard to save a child or facing shocking situations in the ER of a large city hospital, you are right there, in the moment, standing side-by-side with the newly minted physician as he faces the frustration, fatigue, and concern that are often hallmarks of this profession.

The good news is that there is also a great deal of joy and well-earned satisfaction when the science and art of expertly practiced medicine succeeds. There are many such stories in *The Cookie Doctor*, as well as a delightful, lovable, cantankerous, and sometimes wicked cast of characters endemic to small, rural farming communities, deftly portrayed with compassion and wisdom.

As a fellow physician and researcher, I can safely say that there may be no other profession that brings one closer to the miracles of life and death, so brilliantly recounted in this deeply touching memoir.

Nicholas V. Perricone, MD
Madison, CT
January, 2014

People, Places, and Things: Author's Note

Every story in this book is true. There are no composite characters, and the dialogues reflect real conversations, to the best of my ability to recall them. In most cases, the names of the people are real, and I have obtained permission from the families, or individuals themselves if living, to share their stories. Much credit is due to the many people who touched my life along the way, and I am proud to honor them here.

Not every episode of my life allows me to be complimentary about some of the obstacles in my path, nor the people involved. Additionally, some of the medical crises in my practice were of a sensitive nature. In the interest of protecting the privacy of some individuals and certain institutions, I have created fictitious names and generalized locations.

Since there are many common historical names in our community, I took the liberty of using one of my hobbies, woodworking, as the solution to concealing identities without inadvertently using someone else's real name. In this manuscript, anytime a fictitious name was required, I substituted for surnames by assigning the names of my favorite woods. When the reader sees a surname like Birch, Oak, Ash, Hickory, Maple, or part of tree like Root or Branch, it is a fake. Stories in which only first names are used are also written to protect the patients' identities. Any actual names of real persons which may have occurred by using this formula in these stories are accidental and do not knowingly represent any known person living or dead.

ACKNOWLEDGMENTS

No one is ever truly alone. It takes at least two people to bring us into this world, and many more to help us get through it. In writing this book, I became keenly aware of how much credit and gratitude that I owed to each one of the wonderful people who helped me along life's path. Those I name here are a few who were pivotal at major crossroads; without their help, loyalty and love, my life may have taken an entirely different pathway.

God has always been my constant companion, the one I turned to, both in times of great need and great joy. To my first family—my parents, grandparents, uncles, aunts and siblings—I owe immeasurable thanks. For my beloved wife, Joanne, and my children, Steven, Patti, Susan and Peter, there are no words that can adequately convey my love and gratitude to them.

Throughout my journey to become a physician, there were many who guided, encouraged and assisted me in moments which are burned into my memory forever. To Dr. Merle B. DeWire, my family physician, my debt is incalculable. He was my role model, my inspiration to become a physician, and my lifelong friend.

I will be forever grateful to many of my teachers, from grade school through medical school, who were supportive and encouraging. I must acknowledge Dr. Wilbur Shenk, and Dr. James Darlington, and Dean Dr. Breidenstein at Franklin and Marshall College, who encouraged my early research efforts.

From my first step onto Hamilton Walk, the influence of the University of Pennsylvania Medical School professionals was profound and lasting. There are too many to name, but I would be remiss if I didn't give special mention to Dr. John Mitchell, Dean of the University School of Medicine, and to Dr. Roy Williams, Dr. Cletus Schwegman, and Doctor I. S. Ravdin. These esteemed physicians each showed a special interest in my academic efforts, and by sharing their own experiences as practitioners, helped me to become a better doctor in more ways than I can express.

I must thank my wonderful office staff. In those early years, as the new doctor in town, and an Italian-Catholic to boot, I relied heavily on these fine women to help me navigate the customs and the language of the community. Doris Sweigart was my first employee. I cannot describe the debt I owe her, for her constant help, immeasurable talent, and tireless efforts. I am also deeply indebted to Gloria Kauffman, my chief nurse, for her commitment and professional excellence. As my practice was ending, Gloria became one of the first physician's assistants (PA) in the United States. To my office nurses, Sandra Bond, Pearl McCarthy, and Ann Porter, I am eternally grateful for their nursing skills, and delightful humor. I also acknowledge the efficiency of all my secretarial workers over the years, for contributing their skills as both telephone technology and medical billing became increasingly complex.

Deepest thanks go to my patients, who showed incredible faith in my ability. They climbed the steps to my office, and sometimes sat endless hours waiting for me to return from an emergency. One by one, each of my patients provided me with the opportunity to do what it was that I became a doctor to do. In helping my fellow man, I was able to lead a purposeful life. I am particularly grateful to Roy Bubbenmoyer, our local historian, and to Anna Bubbenmoyer, wife of Franklin Bubbenmoyer and the daughter of the esteemed statesman and minister, Reverend Frank Ruth, for providing historical insight. I have been abundantly blessed in serving the people of Bernville.

Apart from the experiences that make up the content of this book, I must finally acknowledge the people who initiated the process that created the book you now hold in your hands. My friend and research colleague, author of many bestselling books on aging and beauty, Dr. Nicholas V. Perricone, provided personal introductions at the highest levels of publishing. May God bless you, Nick, in the way He knows best.

Our heartfelt thanks to our editor, Diane Reverand, for whittling down over eighty stories to reveal the theme of obstacles and miracles along my life's path. Surely, both Ms. Reverand and Dr. Perricone are high on the list of miracles that brought about The Cookie Doctor. In the same vein, I thank my grandson, Michael, for his willing partnership in the business end of publishing of this book.

My thanks to my daughter, Patti, with whom I collaborated on this idea for many years before it actually became a manuscript. She worked relentlessly, correcting my rough drafts and making sense out of run-on-sentences. Without her help and input this book would never have been born.

Finally, I must give special thanks to Sue Walmer, my laboratory associate and office manager. Without Sue's competent help and loyalty, I would never have been able to complete so many projects over the course of our years together.

To all those mentioned, and many more whose names do not appear, I am forever in your debt. And you are forever in my prayers.

Peter T. Pugliese, MD
May 5, 2014

CHAPTER 1

A Country Doctor

There were no patients in the waiting room, none the day before, or the day before that. I could not predict when I would see my first patient that week. The year was 1958. I had started my practice of general medicine in Bernville, Pennsylvania, just four weeks earlier. Bernville was a small, rural town populated mostly by German people, commonly known as the Pennsylvania Dutch.

I was sharing office space with the town's local doctor, who had cared for the citizens of Bernville and the surrounding area for ten years. The equipment I had was sparse: my office desk, the diagnostic instruments I used in medical school, and my books. In the month since moving in, I had seen a young boy with a fractured clavicle and a woman with a sprained ankle. That was a modest beginning.

I had fair warning about what to expect. Other more established friends and colleagues had described the trials of waiting for patients to treat. Almost every doctor in private practice has a story of what it is like at the beginning—counting the bricks on the wall of the adjacent building, nodding off, slumped into a chair, or reaching for the ringing phone with high expectations, only to find another insurance salesman on the line. That day, I pulled *Practical Techniques in General Practice* from the shelf to read while I waited. Within moments, the phone rang, and I picked it up. "Dr. Pugliese."

A soft voice said, "Hello, Doctor, this is Ellen."

"Hello, Ellen, what can I do for you?" I asked.

"I am going to throw my children into the well."

Her tone was flat. That is all she said. Nothing in my training prepared me for a call like this. I knew I had to get there as soon as possible. My first thought was for the children. I said the most neutral thing I could, "Ellen, don't do anything until I get there."

She hung up.

Though I did not know this woman's full name or where she lived, I was now responsible for the lives of her children. I did not know how many. The telephone system in the small town of Bernville, Pennsylvania, in the late fifties was primitive. My phone consisted of a box with a bell, a crank, and a combined head and mouthpiece. I had to crank the phone in order to reach the local operator, who would then connect the party whose number I had given her. Most families shared a "party line," which allowed for constant monitoring of neighbors' conversations. Our line, number 5R22, was private, for my office use only. I rang up the operator and asked her who had just called my office.

"Oh . . ." she hesitated, "I wouldn't know . . ." The operator fumbled, obviously trying to avoid being accused of listening in.

"You must know who that was," I insisted. "You connected us. Operator, this is a matter of life or death. Please give me the name of that girl and tell me where she lives."

The operator cleared her throat and said with a lowered voice, "Her name is Ellen, Ellen Birch. She lives on the first road right, first farm on the left-hand side. It sits back slightly from the road. The house is white with green trim."

"Thank you, Operator." Intent on getting to the farm as soon as I could, I grabbed my medical bag, rushed out of the office, jumped into my car, and roared out of town.

The turn I needed was no more than five minutes away, and the Birch farm probably less than a half mile up the road. As I drove, I feared that Ellen Birch had already thrown her children into the well. I prayed to God that the children were still alive and that I would get there in time to save them.

Hand-dug wells can be anywhere from fifteen to sixty feet deep, typically lined with stones and covered with a wood platform. These covers were made to be easily removed, because a bucket of water had to be pulled up to prime the pump whenever it went dry. I did not have a ladder or ropes with me in the car. As far as I knew, there would be no one else there to help. In the days before cell phones, it was hard to summon help.

To my tremendous relief, as I turned into the driveway, I saw a woman holding an infant with a small boy and a girl standing close to her. Ellen was standing about two feet from the well, with a blank expression on her face. The old wooden cover had been pushed to one side. She had slid it to uncover the well.

Ellen was a thin, worn woman who could not have been more than twenty-five years old. Her uncombed black hair hung around her gaunt face. She was dressed in a shapeless, dingy blue housedress and a gray sweater, torn at the shoulder and with missing buttons. Her shoes were mannish, what we called oxfords. She was looking down, with her head turned to the right. Her eyes were sunken.

Observing her made me realize I was dealing with a postpartum psychosis. She appeared to be at the end of her rope. The first thing I had to do was to get Ellen and the children away from the well. I placed myself between the well and the children and said, "Hi, Ellen, I am Dr. Pugliese. How are you?"

"I'm not so good, Doctor," she responded. "I haven't been sleeping much lately, and I am very tired. I just had a baby, and she keeps me up late."

"Ellen, let me take the baby from you," I suggested, "and why don't you and the children sit in my car?" I asked the names of the children and found the older child was a boy named Paul, after his father. His little sister, Sarah, was not yet two, a year younger than Paul. The baby appeared to be about three months old.

As we moved toward the car, I remembered we had no diapers or milk for the baby. I asked Ellen if she could go back to the house to get them.

"Yes, Doctor," she said.

The children stayed quietly next to me, as I watched Ellen walk to her porch and into the farmhouse. Her gait was as slow and deliberate as a soldier walking through a minefield. Ellen, it appeared, had already stepped on a mine.

She came out carrying a diaper bag and a couple of baby bottles with formula. I opened the car door, and she helped the two children into the backseat first, and then she got into the front. "Ellen, can you hold the baby while I drive the car?" I asked once she was settled.

"Yes, give her to me," she said and took the baby from my arms.

As I slid behind the wheel, I thanked God that the children were alive. I had no idea what to do with a psychotic woman and three children.

The boy and girl were very quiet and docile, almost like two little mannequins. As I backed up the car to turn around, I got a really good look at the well. Had Ellen thrown these children into that well, they surely would be dead.

I needed to get Ellen into the psychiatric ward of our local hospital as soon as possible. I was unfamiliar with the legal papers required to have her admitted. I did know her husband had the first legal responsibility for her. I had to reach him and notify the hospital that we would be arriving. I drove back to the office to get to a telephone. I often drove my Ford Economy station wagon over the rugged dirt lanes and uneven back roads that cut through the landscape and connected a spread-out community of farms to the center of town. I had chosen the car because it was roomy and comfortable. The station wagon served as an ambulance more than once when a patient needed to get to the hospital. As I drove, I kept an eye on Ellen next to me and glanced at the children in the rearview mirror.

"Doctor?" Ellen wanted to know where we were going. I told her we were headed to my office so that I could get some medication for her. She nodded her head, accepting our destination.

When we got to the office, I took the baby again and carried her. We moved toward the door, the small children following quietly. I needed to find someone to care for them while I admitted Ellen to the hospital. When I asked Ellen about relatives, I learned that her young family lived with her mother on the farm. Her mother was working in the clothing factory. Ellen did not know the number. With the baby in one arm, I called the operator, who connected me to the factory. I asked to speak to Ellen's mother. My request was refused, because the company did not allow workers to talk on the phone. I explained the situation to the manager, but he did not seem to care. I hung up, defeated.

"Ellen, how about your grandmother?" I asked. "Does she live close to you?"

"Not far," she replied. She said she could show me how to get there. Without taking the time to call ahead to let the grandmother know we were coming, I got everyone back into the car. We drove about four miles down the highway. Ellen gestured to turn at a driveway to a small, tidy house with well-tended flowerbeds and wind chimes on the porch. A slight, gray-haired woman answered my knock. She was surprised and confused by what she saw. She stood there, eyes darting from me to Ellen and then to the children and back again. I explained who I was.

"Mrs. Oak, I am the new doctor in Bernville. Ellen called me this morning with a medical problem, and she needs some help. I was unable to reach her mother at work, so I am bringing the children here to stay with you while I take Ellen to the hospital. Would that be all right?"

An angry voice came from the darkened living room, an elderly man's gravelly rasp. "Who is it, Mary? What the hell do they want?" I assumed it was her husband.

When he came to the door and stood next to his wife, I had a very uncomfortable feeling that this man was not only uncooperative but potentially dangerous. He seemed aggressive. He pushed his wife aside and demanded, "Who the hell are you, and what are you doing with these children?"

As I explained who I was and what I was doing there, he kept his ferret eyes fixed on me. I said in a firm voice, "I need to leave the children here, while I take Ellen to the hospital for admission."

"Why the hell can't you take the children with you to the hospital?" he shot back.

"Children are not allowed in the hospital, so I must leave them here," I explained.

His wife moved forward and took the baby from Ellen and ushered the children into their living room. Ellen just stood there, detached and expressionless. I said good-bye to both grandparents and to little Paul and Sarah. I steadied Ellen until we got into the car, and we were on our way to the ER.

I asked Ellen about her husband, where he worked, and whether we could reach him. "We got married four years ago, and I have had a baby almost every year. Paul doesn't always have work, but right now, he is working at a junkyard for a guy named Joe." She didn't know whether she could reach him by telephone.

I pulled into the emergency area at the Reading Hospital and guided Ellen into the ER. I spoke to the head nurse, explaining the problem. I arranged to take Ellen directly to the psychiatric ward. She was extremely compliant. She seemed to be relieved that she no longer had the responsibility of the children. When we were inside the locked doors of the psychiatric unit, the nurse in charge wanted to know the doctor of record. She asked who would be there to sign Ellen in. I explained I had to get a relative, namely her husband, but I had been unable to reach him. The nurse agreed to admit Ellen on my service and then transfer her to a psychiatrist who agreed to accept her as a patient. I was finally able to take a deep breath.

I reached Paul's boss, Joe. He was extremely pleasant, very accommodating. I explained that Paul's wife was in the hospital without going into the details and that I needed to speak with her husband to get him to come down to the hospital to sign the admission papers.

When Paul got on the phone, it became evident that I was in for serious trouble. I told him that his wife was in the hospital and that he needed to come down to sign some papers. Paul's first response to the news of his wife's emergency hospitalization seemed normal enough. "When's she coming home?"

"I am not sure, Paul. It looks like she will be in here for a couple weeks, at least."

The exchange that followed gave me an indication of why Ellen's frail body and mind may have collapsed after four years and three children with this man.

He grunted and asked, "Well, who's going to fix my eats?"

"Paul!" I tried to cover my shock. "Your wife is very ill. She needs treatment and rest."

"Yes, well, I need my eats," he repeated.

"Paul, you must come down to the hospital and sign these papers."

"I don't have no car to drive down," he objected.

"Let me speak with Joe again, please," I asked.

His boss took the phone, and I asked Joe if he could please drive Paul to the hospital to sign the papers. He said he would do that.

Next, I called Dr. Elmer Horst, head psychiatrist at the hospital, and explained the situation to him, including the fact that Ellen had no insurance. He said that would be all right and that he would accept her as his patient. Once she had been moved to Dr. Horst's service, she was no longer totally my responsibility, but I was up to my ears in the situation. I was morally and legally involved.

That evening, I spoke with Ellen's mother about her daughter's condition. She had already arranged to pick up the children and spend the evening with them. The plan was for the children to stay with her at night and with their great-grandmother during the day. She seemed like a good woman, who was willing to help as much she could. She was even willing to prepare "the eats" for Paul, who was more concerned about his dinner than his wife's condition.

Postpartum depression was not understood in those days. None of the current openness, awareness, or treatment prescribed for today's young mothers existed in the late fifties. Untreated, women who had just given birth could spiral rapidly into a full psychotic break with reality, void of any emotional bond with the newborn. Infanticide, killing the baby, could occur. The worst case I saw was a farm girl who threw her days-old baby into the furnace, explaining that "he was a runt. The runt of the litter always dies." The most beneficial aspect of hospitalization was removing the exhausted, new mother from the burden of child care and household duties. The sleeping pills of the day, Seconal^{TM} for example, provided an effective short-term remedy. Uninterrupted sleep was often enough to restore normal circadian rhythms and hormonal balance for many women.

As days passed, with rest and specialized talk therapy with Dr. Horst, Ellen was returning to her former self. Three weeks after being admitted, she was ready to go home. As she was being discharged, Ellen thanked me for my help. She did not remember very much about the events of the day we admitted her to the hospital. With no need to remind her of those details, I, in turn, thanked her for calling me that day.

After that incident, I could never be near a hand-dug well, open or closed, without thinking of those three children and Ellen. I saw Ellen a few years ago, at the voting booth, where she was working as a volunteer. She greeted me warmly and asked about my family. I asked about her children. They were all married and doing well. Her husband Paul had died five years earlier. I recalled seeing those children around town. All of them grew up to be productive and responsible citizens.

More than fifty years after the day Ellen called my new office, I cannot help thinking about the many factors that had come together to save those children. The neighbor-to-neighbor familiarity of a small town was critical to the happy outcome. Were it not for an antiquated phone system and a nosy operator, those three souls would not be here today.

My path to being a doctor was by no means a direct route. After first setting out to be a priest, then a Marine during World War II, then a college student, then a soldier in the armored division during the Korean War, I became a premedical student and eventually a medical student. It was a long and arduous trip. Along the way, I met the most wonderful and beautiful girl in the world, and by the grace of God, she married me. Through every twist and turn, she was by my side.

This story, though, is not about our lifelong love affair. It is about people, everyday people whom I cared for through their trials, their illnesses, their weaknesses and strength, good times and bad times. It is a story filled with happiness and sadness and all the vicissitudes of life. It is a story of my faith in God, how

I found God, lost him and found him again, and how I know that God loves us more than we could ever imagine. It is also the story of the incredible power of prayer.

Actually, I did not really choose Bernville as a town in which to practice medicine, it just happened to be there. Bernville and I got together, because we needed each other. I fell in love with a stone farmhouse, and Bernville is where it was.

The Indians called the picturesque country around Bernville *Tulpehocken*, meaning "land of the turtles." The rolling hills with rich valleys, the streams, and woodlands are a sylvan paradise. In the spring, the brilliance of the wildflowers and the activity of the wildlife get your blood moving without traditional sulfur and molasses. The activity of the turtles and frogs every spring in the Tulpehocken area always delighted me. When there was still frost on the ground, the Green Peeper would loudly announce his mating call. For my wife Joanne and me, the Green Peeper was a harbinger of spring.

Bernville was a town of about eight hundred people located in Berks County, Pennsylvania, about fifty miles northwest of Philadelphia. The nearest city is Reading, famous for the Reading Railroad on the Monopoly game board, which most players erroneously pronounce "reed-ing railroad." The population of Bernville is mostly of German descent with a few English families and a fair number of families originating in France.

Descendants of these original settlers still lived in the area when I moved to Bernville in 1957. Families from this area had ancestors who served in the American Revolution. Their names became familiar to me: Reber, Geiss, Haag, Winter, Belleman, Filbert, Strauss, Shepler, and Fuchs. Many families in Bernville had been here before 1800. These included the families named Bond, Rentschler, Kline, Balthaser, Schneider, Seyler,

Bashore, Miller, Lutz, Lesher, Delong, Speicher, Himmelberger, Stoudt, Stump, Reed, Spangler, Zerbe, Sonday, Klopp, Klaus, Diefendbach, Shaeffer, Fisher, Fry, and quite a few others.

The residents of Bernville were always suspicious of strangers and did not admit new people into the community willingly or freely. This attitude was passed on by the old-timers. Many longtime residents told me that you were considered a newcomer in Bernville even if your family lived here fifty years or more.

Everyone knew everyone in town as well as a great deal of their business. This aspect of a small community made many of the townspeople close-mouthed about their personal affairs, particularly how much money they earned. One afternoon, there entered into my office a tall, dark-haired man dressed in workmen's clothing, denim jeans and a blue shirt with his name on it. He was a local tradesman whose identity I will keep secret. He did not come to see me for a professional visit, rather, as he stated, it was "a social call." After asking me a lot of questions about myself, he began to tell me a little bit about the people of Bernville, about their particular viewpoint, and how I could best get along with them. It became obvious very early in his conversation that he was obsessed with making money, but equally obsessed with being seen as having an important position in the community.

We were both smoking cigarettes when he leaned forward and said, "Now, everyone in town will know that you are going to make money here. The important thing is not to show it. You must 'poor-mouth' all the time. People are very jealous in Bernville, and they do not like to see other people get ahead. So if you buy a new car, make sure you let everybody know the bank owns the car and the payments are very high. Also, let them know the taxes are killing you and that everything you have in the office is costing an arm and a leg."

He suggested that I never put expensive furniture in the office and that I should keep the outside of the office neat, but plain, without any show of wealth. He then returned to the car.

"Having the right kind of car is important. If you have a very expensive car, people feel that you are robbing them, but if you have a cheap car, they will think that you cannot afford a better car and will wonder why you are not doing well." He suggested I choose a Buick or Pontiac, and avoid Cadillacs. I had purchased my current car, the Ford station wagon, completely on credit without a down payment. I had achieved that through the kindness of Dr. Archibald Judd, a chest surgeon from Hamburg, Pennsylvania, one of the kindest and most competent physicians I have ever known. My visitor assured me that the station wagon would make an appropriate first impression, adding that people would expect me to buy a new car in a few years, and I had to make the right decision.

When we moved there in 1957, the town of Bernville consisted of Main Street and one parallel side street that were intersected by five numbered streets. The town consisted of a bank, three grocery stores, a bakery, a nonprescription drugstore, two doctors' offices, a plumber, two gas stations, two feed mills, an Agway, a farm machinery distributor named Klopp's, Strauss's auto sales, a clothing factory, two bars, a pool hall, a tobacco and candy shop, a funeral parlor and furniture store combined, a soda-fountain restaurant, a post office, and three churches. That was it.

There was no welcome wagon and no orientation committee to greet us, but there were a few kind souls who came to visit us at home. Some people came to my office not as patients but out of curiosity. People in Bernville disliked not being "in the know." The first person to come to visit us was an old-timer named John Rosewood. John was a farmer, who lived just down the road from us. A short, gray-haired man, he wore wire-rimmed glasses. He was dressed in coveralls and knee-high boots. He had a very strong Pennsylvania Dutch accent. We invited him into our living room. The odor of cow manure began to permeate the room, because the bottoms of his boots were caked with the stuff. We could not think of a polite way to usher him out, so we sat captive for almost two hours listening to his life story and tales about Bernville. I remember him telling us that he had gone to college for one month. He did have a lot of information about our farm. According to John, ours was the only stone-gabled barn in Jefferson Township. Finally, John took his leave for the evening milking, bid us good-bye, and said he would come again. We told him he was welcome. I don't know how sincere we sounded.

Remembering some of my early experiences with the Pennsylvania Dutch still brings a smile to my lips. Lloyd Himmelberger and Oscar Rentschler, two of my older male patients, taught me some of the local dialect, under the guise of helping me to communicate better with the Pennsylvania Dutch patients. It turned out that those two rascals were actually teaching me German vulgarities and enjoying a good laugh at the expense of the rookie doctor. Lloyd and Oscar were longtime friends, both retired farmers. They lived in Churchtown, a single street near the north end of Bernville, so named because the main road went down and up a gully on the other side of the Lutheran Church. Lloyd was a widower who had remarried. Lloyd lived in a substantial house. Oscar lived in a trailer immediately across the street from him. Since Lloyd no longer drove, Oscar would transport him on his errands. They always scheduled their doctor appointments together. Some of the most embarrassing moments of my life can be attributed to these two pranksters. I took care of them for many years, and once I learned what they were up to, I was able to sidestep their tricks.

The first prank they played on me involved a stomach preparation that they called "esel sake." (AY sawl SAYk). Lloyd had an upset stomach, and he asked if I had any of this particular stomach remedy. When I said I did not know what it was, he said, "Naaah, Doc, you call Dr. Nagel in Wernerswille once. He vill tell you where you can get it." I quickly learned the letters v and w were interchangeable in spoken Pennsylvania Dutch, and "once" was said often and randomly and cannot be grammatically explained or correlated to anything in any other language. Another baffling expression, "what I mean" was repeated as the Dutchman's equivalent of "you know." *"Vell, Doc, what I mean, it gives me pain what I mean when I go, what I mean when I have to go sometimes I can't go, what I mean and why then I have this pain."*

Arlly Nagel was a fellow general practitioner from Wernersville, a slightly larger town bisected by Route 422, a main artery that ran from the farmlands all the way to Philadelphia. Arlly told me I could get the product at Bamford's Medical Supply and gave me the item number to ask for when I called them. He said it was an antispasmodic with a sedative and would work well for a number of stomach disorders associated with indigestion. I ordered it, and soon a gallon jug of a thick yellow liquid arrived with a formulation that I recognized as an old-time remedy for gastric distress. Both Lloyd and Oscar swore by this medication.

One day, Mabel Ash, a diminutive seventy-year-old lady, came in the office complaining of postprandial acid indigestion. After examining her, I suggested some changes in her diet and offered to give her effective medication known as esel sake. She gave me a look that I shall never forget and reluctantly took the medication with her. She looked back at me a couple of times as she left the office. I did not understand her reaction. Several days later, I suggested this remedy to another patient, a robust male of forty-five. He laughed out loud when I told him the name of the medication.

"Vell, himmel, if you say it's good, Doc, I'll take it." He too left the office shaking his head.

31

I had seen the confusion in my patients' reaction. I asked the next patient, who spoke "Dutch," the meaning of esel sake.

He let out a hearty laugh and said, "Why do ask that question, Doctor?"

I explained that it was old-time medicine that Lloyd Himmelberger and Oscar Rentschler recommended that I stock for stomach aches. He laughed again, and I couldn't believe my ears when he said, "Vell, nah, Doctor, 'esel sake' means 'mule piss.'"

They got me once again.

One afternoon, when Lloyd and Oscar came in, I surprised them with the German expression I had mastered, *Wie geht es du?* which in the Pennsylvania Dutch pronunciation sounds like "vee gates do" and means "How are you?" Since I had learned that greeting, they suggested that I use an alternate expression as well. They enthusiastically taught me to say, *Wie hangen du, auf oden hinab?* When I asked them what this meant, they said it was another friendly greeting, sort of like saying, "How does it go with you?"

I practiced it a few times with them until I had the accent correct. I was proud to add this expression to my PA German vocabulary, which by that time consisted of approximately fifty words, most of them anatomical.

The next morning, in walked a little old lady whom I had known for some years, whose name was Edna Maple. Enthusiastically, I wished her a good morning with my new expression, "*Guten Morgen, Edna. Wie hangen du, auf oden hinab?*"

She looked at me with absolute astonishment and sniffed indignantly, "Well, Doctor, I never! Who told you to say that?"

"Oscar Rentschler and Lloyd Himmelberger told me it was a friendly greeting," I replied, sheepishly.

"Well, it is a terrible thing to say to anyone, let alone a woman!" she chided.

I apologized profusely and finished her exam, not wanting to insult her further by asking what I had actually said to her.

When Arlen, a Pennsylvania Dutch-speaking patient, came in after lunch, I asked him what my new sentence meant. He chuckled and asked me why I wanted to know. I explained that my Dutch language coaches, Oscar and Lloyd, advised me to use this greeting. I told him of my horrifying exchange with Mrs. Maple. His eyes flew open wide and he exclaimed, "Ach my, noooowah, Doc!"

After Arlen finished a belly laugh at my expense, he said, "Doc, this is what men say to each other who are good friends and have known each other for a long time. It means in English, 'How does it hang, up or down?' and of course, refers to the penis."

I had the urge to strangle both of those rascals the next time they came to the office.

When I saw them again, I told them what had happened when I tried to impress Edna during her visit. The two of them laughed uproariously, throwing their heads back and slapping their thighs and choking until tears came to their eyes. I had to laugh myself, but I wised up. Any expression from those two devils got translated before I used it.

The Pennsylvania Dutch dialect continued to stump me. One of my first housecalls was on the road to Rehrersburg. I got a phone call one evening about a man with abdominal pain.

His wife told me that he had a little "ernie" that would come out every now and then and give him trouble, but she could usually put it back in. That afternoon, she was not able to get it back in. I had no idea what an "ernie" was, so I asked her about its location. After she explained, I suspected it was an inguinal hernia. I asked her to describe it. She said it was about the size of a golf ball but was getting hard and turning blue. It sounded like a strangulated hernia that needed immediate attention. She told me she lived in Bessel. I had not heard of Bessel, so I inquired if it was anywhere near Rehrersburg, and she happily said, "Yes, it's the next town."

"Good," I replied, "is it near Bethel?"

Confused, she said, "Why, Doc, Bessel is Bessel." Only then did I realize that this was another pronunciation I had to learn. I zipped up to "Bessel" (dipthongs be damned), examined her husband Clarence, called Dr. Davis, and shipped my patient down to him for appropriate surgery.

Clarence's wife was one of the most "Dutchified" women I had ever met. I learned later from her that when a wound was "burning dirt" it was suppurating or making pus. When the pain was ill-defined, it was frequently described as "a dumbness."

The language moment that gave me the greatest laugh was when a woman called me on Saturday afternoon, asking me to come up to see her husband who was hurt in the crotch.

"Could you come to the office?" I asked, not wanting to drive seventeen miles for a housecall on a Saturday afternoon.

"*Vhy, noooowah,* Doctor, he can't," she said excitedly, "the whole crotch roof is lying on top of him!" Only then did I understand she was talking about a *garage* roof. Her husband and his friend had been demolishing an old garage by pulling it down with a little tractor. Her husband ended up trapped under the garage roof. I drove to their farm with my son Peter, who was twelve at the time. When we arrived, we saw that the man was indeed trapped under the roof. Fortunately, we were able to extricate him from the debris. He suffered only two small lacerations and a bruised hip and shoulder. I was thankful he had no serious injury.

I was making a housecall to a seventy-eight-year-old farmer named Roy who had been sick for more than a week with what the Pennsylvania Dutch called "a heavy cold." His wife had been treating him with a fried onion poultice, a flannel cloth impregnated with camphorated oil around his neck, and Vicks VapoRub™ up his nostrils. The odor of fried onions, menthol, and camphorated oil was noxious. The patient was upstairs in a small bedroom that was heated by a kerosene space heater. The stifling heat and the added odor of the kerosene made the room a small hell. His wife, Alma, was hard of hearing, and she assumed everyone else had the same affliction. Standing a foot away from me, she spoke with an exceptionally loud, explosive voice. I approached the bed, put down my bag, and took out my stethoscope. Upon opening Roy's shirt, I had to brush aside the fried onions and melted Vicks from his chest. It was a mess. Alma objected loudly to what I was doing. She believed that disturbing her remedies would seriously affect his condition. I persisted, ignoring her shouts. I asked her to be quiet, so I could listen to his chest. His color was poor, and his breathing was shallow and rapid. He had either a solid lobar pneumonia or empyema. With her help, I was able to sit him up and percuss, or tap on, his chest. There was fluid in his lower chest, most likely pus.

I took a 50-ml syringe and a twenty-gauge needle from my medical bag. After cleansing the skin with alcohol, I made a puncture on the lateral part of his chest between two ribs. I aspirated a dirty, yellow pus, taking out about 40 ml. I asked his wife for a basin and some towels. He had a liter or more of pus in his chest. She brought the basin and two hand towels. I put on a pair of latex surgical gloves. With a number eleven blade, I made a one-inch incision between his ribs. I knew it would hurt, but there was no time to apply local anesthetic. I inserted a scalpel handle to pry open the wound and collected copious quantities of pus in the basin. By the time the basin was nearly full, his breathing had improved considerably, and he started to talk again.

I told him that he would have to go to the hospital for additional treatment. He could not understand why, because he felt better. I explained to him that he was a long way from being cured and that he probably would have to have more fluid removed from his chest. He definitely needed an x-ray and a culture of the pus so that he could start taking proper antibiotics. He was resistant, and his wife made a fuss. She thought a stay at the hospital was unnecessary. It did not take long to persuade her that her husband had been near death and that he needed additional treatment. We called an ambulance. She sent her daughter with her husband to the hospital to help with the admission. Apparently, she was embarrassed by her hearing disability.

After I packed my bag, I had a cup of coffee in the kitchen with Alma and further explained the seriousness of her husband's condition. I told her I was glad that she called when she did, because within another twenty-four hours, there was a high probability that her husband would have died. Along with the coffee, she gave me an excellent piece of apple pie. I never ceased to be surprised by the Pennsylvania Dutch. While they sometimes could be cold and downright impolite, it was endearing to me when they revealed their inherent shyness and humility.

The people of Bernville were a diverse group. There were a few specialty farms that raised chickens and pigs, but the majority of the families were engaged in dairy farming. Dairy farming is highly labor-intensive, subject to many variables.

You could say I had grown up in the dairy business. At one time, my father's trucking business included every dairy in the Berks County area but one. From the time I was in third grade, I worked with my dad on the milk truck, as did my two older brothers. We hauled milk from the dairy farms to the dairy plants where it was processed, bottled, and distributed. We were up at 4:00 a.m., out in the country until 7:00 a.m., heading to the dairy plants in time to deliver the milk. We raced to grade school by 8:30 a.m. This was my childhood routine, seven days a week. On Sunday, I had to get back in time to serve Mass as an altar boy. I knew many of the Bernville farmers as a young boy and as a teenager, because they were part of our milk route. They were surprised to have me show up as a doctor many years later. This background in the dairy business helped me to establish a rapport with many of the farmers. Though I could not speak Pennsylvania Dutch, I knew enough about the dairy business to speak that same language. My childhood experience in the dairy business was to prove invaluable in my work as a doctor.

There was not a Catholic church in the Bernville area. Since I had to go either to Reading or to Hamburg to attend Mass, I could not mix with the non-Catholic population on Sunday morning. It took me a while to realize that there was a very strong prejudice against Catholics in Bernville and the neighboring towns. Catholic physicians were believed to be willing to kill a pregnant mother in order to save the baby. Other Catholic doctors told me that no amount of explanation would ever dispel this myth.

One of my longtime patients stopped by to ask me if I would recommend a doctor for her in Shoemakersville, where she was moving. I recommended Dr. Christ, an excellent physician in every way. When I mentioned his name, her eyes widened.

"He is a Catholic!" she exclaimed.

I told her that I was also Catholic and had been treating her for a decade.

She looked at me in amazement. Smiling, she said she would start seeing Dr. Christ.

A good part of my practice was made up of Mennonites, who are Christians. Their name is taken from Menno Simons, a Dutch priest who had converted to the Anabaptist faith, in which adult believers were baptized. Mennonites believe in the close textual readings of the Scriptures. They are known for their emphasis on peace, justice, simplicity, community, service, and mutual aid. One of the cornerstones of the Mennonite faith is pacifism. All the young men elected to serve the community during wartime rather than go into the military service.

The Mennonites were mainly from Swiss and German roots. Many older Mennonites continued to speak a German dialect called "Plautdietsch" and ate traditional foods. The sense of community in the Mennonites' lives deeply impressed me. Their family gatherings were very large, involving many neighbors and friends, some of whom traveled a great distance to attend. The three families with whom I had the most contact were the Longeneckers, the Weavers, and the Snyders.

While making a housecall to see a senior member of the Longenecker family, Mrs. Mead, the matriarch, and I were discussing a celebration planned for the wedding anniversary of one of her grandchildren. It sounded like quite an affair with guests from just about everywhere. In an offhand remark, I mentioned that Joanne and I had never had a wedding anniversary celebration that involved anyone but the two of us. The next year, Mrs. Mead arranged a surprise celebration for our thirteenth anniversary. I don't remember how many people were there, but there were mountains of presents. I cannot adequately describe the love expressed by those people. They were true friends. For four generations, they have continued to be close to our family.

The Amish settled mostly about thirty miles from Bernville in Lancaster County. Known as the Old Order Amish, or the horse-and-buggy Amish, they still farm with horse power and continue to drive buggies to church services and into town. When I worked at St. Joseph's Hospital in Lancaster, I had many Amish as patients. I found them friendly and very kind. I was invited to their homes and shared some of their meals. They are among the most efficient, hardworking people I have ever met, as well as the happiest. They live well-ordered lives filled with work and love. There surely is something to say for that simple way of living.

The Pennsylvania Dutch are famous for their foods, not only the quality but the quantity. Thinness is not admired by the Pennsylvania Dutch. Obesity and diabetes were two diseases I had to battle constantly in my patients. Being overweight is considered by many of them to be a sign of affluence and health. Imagine how hard it was to try to change that attitude. When making housecalls, I was often invited to join the family for a meal. The breakfast of a Pennsylvania Dutchman was legendary. At one farm, where I happened to be stuck in a snowdrift, the farmer invited me for breakfast before he pulled my car from the snow with his tractor. The breakfast consisted of fried eggs, fried potatoes, and sausage. This was followed by pancakes and scrapple, a butcher-scrap specialty whose ingredients are best left un-itemized. The mixture is ground up, formed into a loaf, sliced, dredged in flour, fried, and served covered with maple syrup. Finally, coffee was accompanied by coconut cake. I estimate that I had consumed close to three thousand calories that morning. No wonder I was facing an uphill battle against obesity in the Pennsylvania Dutch.

Country doctors are often paid in commodities. The farmers were generous with gifts of seasonal produce and their butchered meats, providing us with an abundance of smoked sausages, hams for Easter dinner, and fresh turkeys at Thanksgiving. As for baked goods, every Pennsylvania Dutch wife had her own recipe for shoo-fly pie, a heavy confection of molasses, lard, sugar, and "wet-bottom" piecrust.

I was particularly fond of Lepp cookies, which were waiting for me at the home of one particular family whenever I made a housecall there.

After I'd been in practice a few years, I got a call from my friend Bob Donovan, a quiet intellectual, from my medical school class at the University of Pennsylvania. He expressed an interest in moving away from the city and perhaps practicing in a rural area as I did. I invited him to bring his wife, Barbara, and stay with us for a few days so that he could see for himself. He accompanied me on a housecall to Mr. Hickory, a longtime smoker with emphysema. My patient was having difficulty breathing, or as his wife said, "His air is shutting off again." When I first saw him as a patient, I understood that there had been some financial hardship in their family, but they were pleasant, and their home was always clean and welcoming with the aroma of something in the oven. I quietly established a barter arrangement with them for my fees.

The dirt lane was rutted with a collection of old tires off to one side and a tractor up on blocks near the barn. A young boy in muddy denim pants saw us approaching and ran toward the house. Mrs. Hickory stood holding open the screen door. The smell of fresh baked cookies greeted us as we entered the warm kitchen.

"Hello, Doctor!" she called. As she ushered us in to the living room where her husband was sitting, the boy appeared. He listened while I introduced Bob to his parents. "This is Dr. Donovan, and he is going to be working with me." As Bob pulled his stethoscope from his pocket and listened to Mr. Hickory's chest, the boy's eyes narrowed, obviously sizing up this newcomer. He looked nervously from his mother to his father, to me, and back to Bob. He rose up to his full height and confronted Bob with a serious question.

"Are you a real doctor who wants money? Or are you a cookie doctor like Dr. Pugliese?"

Chapter 2

Housecall on Horseback

It was a bitter cold winter with a lot of snow blowing and temperatures below zero. Housecalls became increasingly difficult as the lanes drifted shut. Even the highways were sometimes impassable. The snow seemed to remain on the ground forever. I dreaded the thought of late-night housecalls with the prospect of being stuck halfway down a long lane. There was no way to communicate if I did get stuck.

The first snow to hit us in November began as a light flurry and gradually picked up in tempo. By nightfall, the snow was more than four inches and beginning to drift. When I finished with my last patient at about 10:00 p.m., it was difficult to drive from the office down the lane. I got stuck in drifts several times. By jockeying the car, a four-wheel-drive Scout, I was able to break through the drifts. I was happy to be home with my family, snug and safe in a warm house. The night wore on and the storm raged. The wind howled and beat against the windows, banged some of the shutters, and began to pile snow against the doors. It was going to be a terrible night. Since we could not get any television reception, we sat around the fireplace roasting chestnuts and telling stories.

The telephone rang two or three times. One patient called to cancel an appointment for the morning. The second call was from a young mother, whose two-year-old son had what she described as "a chest cold." She said he was breathing all right but had a deep cough. I told her to call me if he got any worse, particularly if his color changed or he lost his voice. This boy had either bronchitis or tracheal bronchitis, but there was no way I could get to him during this blizzard. I said we should wait to see what the morning brought in. I would try to find a way to get out to the highway and come up to see him the next day. We left it at that, but the delay gave me cause for concern.

We went to bed early that night. All the children were tucked in, and my wife and I were in bed by 11:30. As we fell asleep, we could hear the wind picking up and the icy snow slamming against the windows. The ringing phone interrupted my sleep. As I reached for the receiver, I noticed it was two o'clock in the morning. It was Mrs. Beech calling about her little boy, reporting that his breathing was worse and his color did not look good. There was no advice I could give her except to make a steam bath. I instructed her how to do this. "Take a teapot of water, and heat it on an electric plate. Make a small tent with a towel to help retain the steam around the baby's head."

I said I would be there in the morning. She was silent. I told her I could not get there because of the weather. The roads were drifted shut, even if I was able to get out of my lane. She said she was terribly worried about the boy and hung on to the phone. There was nothing else I could say and no way for me to get any medication to her. I felt stymied. I was concerned about the little boy. Croup, or laryngotracheobronchitis, could be fatal, especially for a child that age.

Then I thought of Bill.

When my son, Steven, was eight years old, I decided to buy a horse to teach him to ride. One of my patient friends trained horses and taught riding. She had a large and gentle Morgan she was willing to sell me, along with a saddle and a hackamore, a bridle without a mouth bit. Bill was an eight-year-old gelding. He had never been accustomed to a bridle and would only accept the hackamore. She saddled him up, and I rode him around the barnyard. He had been trained to neck rein and was three-gaited. Mary Jane delivered Bill that afternoon. She threw in free riding lessons for my son. Stevie and Bill got along well. In no time, he was riding around the farm without a saddle, sometimes with his little four-year-old sister, Patti, holding onto his back. Steve and I spent many hours that summer riding Bill and exploring nooks and crannies of our farm.

Our horse would not be happy about going out into this weather. I did not know if I could manage him. He had a mind of his own and could become difficult to handle. I had some experience at riding, but I certainly was not an expert horseman. I called Mrs. Beech and told her that I was going to try to get there as soon as I could. She thanked me and went to set up the steam bath.

Joanne could not believe that I was going to do this. "You can't go out in the storm! You have never ridden Bill in this kind of weather, or at nighttime. What if he bucks you off and you're lying somewhere on the road hurt? No one will be able to find you!" she said, pleading.

"Honey," I said, "I must do this. It is the only chance this baby is going to have to live."

"But you might die trying!" she insisted.

"Please don't worry . . . it should be all right. I will pray for protection and do the best I can."

Our home was a half a mile from the highway. The snowdrifts were higher than six feet, and up near the highway, they were even higher. The lane was still a dirt road that twisted and dipped as it wound its way back to the farmhouse. With this kind of snow, the lane was completely impassable. There was no other way out to the highway. The highway was also covered with drifts. No one was on the road.

Having dressed as warmly as I could, I checked my bag to make sure I had the necessary steroids and antibiotics. I put a strong belt through the handles of my medical bag to hang it onto the saddle. I had to push my way out the front door through a three-foot drift and make my way down to the barn. When I arrived at the barn, Bill took one look at me, and I knew we were going to have a problem.

I got the hackamore on him. When it came to putting the saddle on, he blew himself up and started to go through his tricky dance routine, which made it very difficult to get the saddle on him. I yanked on the hackamore a couple times, told him to be still, but he was not about to obey. After three attempts, I finally got the saddle snugly fastened, took him out of the barn, and mounted him. The medical bag strapped onto the saddle horn was in the way of my leg, but there was nothing I could do about it. We started out of the barnyard and up the road past the house. He was snorting all the while to let me know that this was a stupid thing to do and that he should be back in the barn. I urged him on.

I was amazed by how cold I was, sitting on a horse with the wind blowing over me. I had no protection for my face. My ears were stinging. Even though I was wearing gloves, my fingers were becoming numb in just a short distance. I had a little more than a mile to go to reach the village of New Schaefferstown. I wasn't sure what the best route would be because of the drifting we encountered. Taking the lane up to my neighbor Russell's house seemed the best way to go. It was protected by a double row of locust trees. The drifts were not too high there. We were able to make good progress. Once we passed Russell's farm, I headed for the highway. At the highway, it became apparent that the drifts would make it impassable. I had to stick to the high ground, mainly the fields on either side of the road. We traveled about a quarter mile on the top of one field and then ran into a drift. I had to search for an opening to get to the other side of the highway. Bill tried to turn back. I had to fight him all the way, my cold hands becoming increasingly numb.

I tried to avoid the really deep areas. I knew plowing through the deep snow would tire Bill out, and then I would really have a problem with him. My face had lost all of its feeling. Ice was forming on my gloves and on my hat. I pulled my scarf up a little higher to cover my mouth, but soon gave up on this. The moisture from my breath froze, making my face even colder. I hit a lucky patch of highway. The snow had blown off the highway completely, forming a huge drift on the other side. My only concern was that the road might be slippery for Bill. We made our way very carefully. We were about a half mile from New Schaefferstown when the snow began to grow deeper. There were houses on both sides of the highway. It was difficult to find high ground. We had to push through high drifts. I could see the lights from New Schaefferstown through the driving snow, a very welcome sight. The last quarter mile was the toughest, because the snow had drifted in the main street and piled heavily against the houses. When I reached the Beech's house, the front porch, which was at street level, was covered with three or four feet of snow. I tied Bill to one of the posts holding the porch roof. The husband shouted through the door to come to the side door, because they couldn't get the front door open. The way to the side door was clear, and they were waiting for me when I got there.

The sensation of being in a warm house, after almost an hour in driving, freezing snow, is beyond description. It seemed like paradise just to be warm. The baby was downstairs in a crib, and they were applying the steam tent. Mrs. Beech said that the baby had improved slightly with the steam, but she was still worried. I warmed my hands as best I could, got my stethoscope, and examined his chest. He was not moving air at all. His color was really bad, not an ashen gray, but he was not pink either. His throat was red and swollen. His ears were not infected. He was seriously ill. Without proper treatment, he might have died. I gave him an injection of Decadron™, which reduced the laryngeal swelling, and his breathing improved tremendously. Then I gave him antibiotics orally. The new oral forms of penicillin were as rapid-acting as an intramuscular injection. After that, all we could do was to wait. It was a little after 3:30 in the morning. I asked Mrs. Beech for a cup of coffee. She said she would make a pot.

I sat and talked with her husband as we drank coffee and lit cigarettes. Then it occurred to me that any tobacco smoke could be detrimental to the baby, and I suggested we both stop smoking. Mr. Beech was amazed that I was able to get to their house even on horseback. He said that this had to be one for the books, because doctors had not made housecalls on horseback since the 1920s. He recalled his father telling him stories when he was a boy, of how the local doctor from Bernville made housecalls in a horse and buggy. With the snow in the wintertime, he came on horseback. He told me about the saddlebags the doctors used that were slung over the horse's neck in front of the saddle. That was a good idea, keeping the bag from banging against his leg.

I stayed with the Beeches until dawn. After I listened to the little boy's chest and heard that he had a good airway, I was happy. Between 5:30 and 6:00 a.m., I decided the little boy was safe, and I could head for home. I left instructions for Mrs. Beech on how to give the antibiotic and left her some syrup of Ipecac. As I got back into my warm clothes, I asked them to call me in about three hours. When I ventured out into the cold morning air, I found that the snow had stopped and the wind had subsided.

Bill was covered with ice crystals. He was not a happy camper. When I came out, he snorted to express his displeasure about standing out in the cold all night. I knocked the ice from the saddle, mounted, and started back home. Someone had plowed a small opening in the middle of the main street out to the main road which made getting out of town a breeze compared to getting there. When we reached the main road, we were in trouble again. The height of the drifts was apparent in the dawn's early light. Highway 419 was an absolute mess. I had to zigzag my way from house to house along 419 until I reached Highway 183.

It took me more than half an hour of pushing and climbing and plowing until we reached the main road. There, before my eyes, was a clear highway with only a few inches of snow and no drifts as far as I could see down the road. I had trouble holding Bill down. He wanted to go faster. I knew that he would fall on the ice, as he was not experienced with slippery roads. I had to rein him in constantly. He was snorting and occasionally made a feeble buck. I yelled at him to settle down. When we reached Russell's lane, the dawn had broken into a beautiful sunrise. We climbed some banks to get onto the high ground on the side of Russell's lane that took us directly home.

As soon as we made the turn into the lane that joined Russell's place and our farm, Bill broke into a run. The medical bag was flopping so fiercely, I was afraid it would break loose from the strap. I was holding the bag to the saddle horn and trying to rein in Bill. We hit a drift that stopped him in his tracks. He was forced to make slow progress. He pushed his way through the drifts, past our house, and down to the barn. I dismounted outside the barn and removed his saddle and hackamore. He ran into the barn. He had done a good job, so I gave him an extra ration of honey bran oats, four extra ears of corn, and an extra fork full of hay.

Carrying my bag, I made my way across the barnyard and up to the house. There was a huge drift in front of the door which I had pushed through when I left the previous night. Now I was faced with it again. I kicked as much of the snow away from the bottom of the door as I could. My wife appeared at the door with an enormous smile and relief on her face. She pushed from the inside, and I pulled the door. We finally made an opening big enough for me to get in. She threw her arms around me, kissed me, and hugged me and cried with joy that I was safe.

"Gosh," I said, "the old-time doctors did this all the time. It was really nothing for them to make housecalls with snow and rain . . ." but I couldn't finish.

Joanne just hung on to me and said she was so happy that I was all right. "Please promise me you will never do this again." This was my Joanne. This was the woman that I loved. This was my wife, and my very best friend.

"I am really hungry," I said. "I would like some fried eggs, a little scrapple or bacon, and some fried potatoes."

"I would, too," she said. "The kids are still sleeping, so I will get it together."

After we finished eating, I made a fire in the fireplace, put my feet up, and relaxed. I knew there would be no office hours that day. I was praying there would be no more housecalls. As I sat before the fire, I thanked God that the little boy had responded and that I had made it home safely. I thanked Him also for my beautiful and loving wife.

Some years later, I purchased two "snowmobiles" for the children. On one occasion, I made a housecall on this new snow-traversing vehicle. I never again made a housecall on horseback.

CHAPTER 3

Divine Interventions

My entire life has been a search to understand the relationship between the physical and the spiritual. My friendship with my patient Ernie gave me great insight, inspiration, and affirmed my beliefs.

Ernie and his wife Molly were patients for almost fifteen years. During the time I took care of them, neither had a serious medical problem. Ernie had moderate hypertension, for which he came to the office religiously every two to three months to have his blood pressure checked and his medications refilled. He was not a big man, just about five foot six and did not weigh more than 140 pounds. He had worked in a feed mill for forty years. A religious man, he was socially active in the Rotary Club and an avid member of the local volunteer fire department, proud that he had been one of the early members of the organization. Country towns as a rule do not have paid community services like fire departments. They rely entirely on the volunteer citizens to supply the service. When the fire department had a fund-raising breakfast, Ernie could usually be seen at the griddle, smiling and flipping pancakes.

He wore small, wire-framed glasses. I think he was as self-conscious about his glasses as he was about his height. The men at the mill told me that Ernie always volunteered for the most demanding work, particularly lifting heavy bags of feed on and off a truck. He prided himself on his strength.

Every time he came to the office, he would bring me a little gift, usually candy—licorice or gummies he purchased at the local farmer's market where he went every Thursday evening. When he talked, he had a habit of rubbing his right hand through his shock of wavy gray hair. When he was very serious and had something important to say, he would remove his glasses, look you straight in the eye, and make his point. Ernie would start off just about every visit by telling me a joke that usually involved a Pennsylvania Dutchman.

"Why, Doc, did ya hear the one about the Dutchmen on the phone? The phone rang at 1:30 in the morning. The weary Dutchman crawled from his bed to get the phone, and answered, 'Helloowah!'"

A voice on the other end asked, kind of confused, "Is this numbah 111 (vun vun vun)?"

"Vhy, noooo-ah," responded the sleepy guy, "This is numbah 1-11 (vun eleven)!"

"ACH!" said the caller, "I am so sorry to get you up!"

"Vell," the guy tells him, "it's okayah. I had to get up to answer the phone anyhow!"

Patients like Ernie not only brightened my day but also made me feel good about being a physician.

Every now and then, a patient would tell me that he was going to die and would name the disease. When asked how he knew, the patient usually replied that he was not sure. He just felt it was going to happen. Such was the case with Ernie. For the past three years, he had come to my office asking for an upper GI x-ray. He was certain he was going to die of stomach cancer. Ernie was not a worrier, so his concern about stomach cancer surprised me. There was no history of stomach cancer in his family. In fact, the only case of cancer of which he was aware was on his wife's side of the family. For three consecutive years, he appeared at the office after the first of the year and asked me to schedule an x-ray for him. He wanted to get it over with and have an answer for the rest of the year. I tried to explain to him that he was exposing himself to a large dose of radiation, which was not good for him. He was insistent, and I went along with it.

When the x-ray report came to the office, I was surprised to see the presence of gallstones and some obstruction to the flow of bile. I thought that Ernie probably would be pleased, because we found something wrong with him. I called him to tell him there was a positive finding and asked him to come to the office to discuss the x-rays and the need for more studies. He made an appointment for the next day. He was cheerful when he came in, but he was reticent in a way that was not like the Ernie I knew.

"Ernie," I began, "the x-ray shows that you have gallstones and that there is a certain amount of obstruction to the flow of bile. You have a blockage-of-the-gallbladder problem, most likely due to the stones."

"Are you sure, Doctor, that's all there is, just gallstones?"

"Well, Ernie, as far as we can tell, that's all that the x-ray shows. You will have to have surgery to remove the gallstones to get rid of the blockage of your gallbladder."

"Okay, Doc, I guess we might as well get the surgery over and have done with it."

"Good," I said, "I will call Dr. Davis and get you scheduled as soon as possible."

Ernie left the office more resigned than happy about the discussion. There was something subtle in his attitude that appeared fatalistic to me. I found out later that he told his wife, Molly, that he had something really bad and that I just wasn't telling him about it. He wanted to get his things in order before going to the hospital.

Ernie had an appointment to see my friend, a skilled surgeon named Dr. Arnold V. Davis, the subsequent week. The surgery was scheduled three days later. Based on the x-rays, Dr. Davis felt that this routine gallbladder and stone removal would relieve the obstruction. I called Ernie and told him that Dr. Davis agreed with the x-ray finding and felt this would be a routine procedure. I assured Ernie that he would be up and about in a matter of a few weeks.

Ernie insisted that Dr. Davis was going to find more wrong with him at the time of the surgery. He doubted very much whether he would ever leave the hospital. I tried to reassure him and told him he was worried needlessly. He didn't have stomach cancer, just plain, ordinary gallstones.

"Yes, well, Doctor," he replied, "I guess we just have to wait and see."

The afternoon following surgery, I received a call from Dr. Davis. During surgery, he discovered that Ernie had metastatic carcinoma of the ampulla of Vater, the site where the pancreatic duct and the common bile duct join. It is about halfway down the duodenum. This is a rare form of cancer that was totally inoperable. Dr. Davis said he was going to wait until that evening to talk to Ernie about what he had found. He was not quite sure how to break the news to Ernie, because his life expectancy would be relatively short. I told Dr. Davis that Ernie had a premonition for years that he was going to die of stomach cancer. In many ways, he was prepared for this diagnosis and eventuality.

About 9:30 that night, I had to admit another patient to the hospital with a critical illness. After he was admitted and his course of therapy was planned, I went over to the surgical ward to see Ernie. He was still awake, with nasal suction and IVs running, lying in his bed looking much smaller than I had ever seen him.

"Hi, Ernie, how is it going?"

"Dr. Davis was here a few minutes ago and explained to me what I have. It is pretty bad. I probably have less than six months to live. What do you think?"

"From what Dr. Davis told me this afternoon on the telephone, I agree with him that this is a pretty bad situation, but I'm not sure about how long you have to live, Ernie. We know for certain that this tumor cannot be treated with surgery alone. We can possibly use chemotherapy to beat it down, but I don't think we can cure it."

I waited for his response. He looked at me in a way that communicated he knew far more about this than I did and that he was going to die a lot sooner than I thought. I felt terrible that I could do nothing medically to help this dying man. He was not only one of my favorite patients, but we had been friends for more than fifteen years. The thought of him dying this horrible death was devastating to me.

Finally, he looked directly at me in that intense way of his and said, "You know, Doctor, I knew this was coming. Remember three years ago when I told you I was going to die of stomach cancer? Well, this may not be stomach cancer, but it sure is close."

I wanted to ask Ernie how he knew this, what gave him this premonition, and why he felt so sure that he was going to die of cancer, but I hesitated to do it. Instead, I said, "Ernie, I'm going to have a cancer specialist see you to find out if there are new types of chemical compounds we can use to treat this type of cancer. Researchers are working on new things every day, and some of the discoveries are more effective than they were a few years ago. The specialist will see you in the morning and discuss what else we can do."

"Yes, well, Doctor, if you think it might help. But I don't think it will do any good," Ernie responded, matter-of-factly.

I told Ernie I would see him in the morning, that I would remember him in my prayers, and that I was sure his church would be praying for him as well.

I did not make it to see him the next morning, but the oncologist did. He did not suggest chemotherapy for Ernie, because the tumor was so far spread. At that time, there really wasn't anything that would be effective. I did not want to give him five-fluorouracil, the drug used in those days, because it had such a devastating effect on all the normal tissue. Late that afternoon, when I made hospital rounds, I stopped to see Ernie. We discussed what the oncologist had told him. I sat and talked with him a few minutes. I had to go to the university in Philadelphia the next day and would not be able to see him. I explained that Dr. Davis would see him every day to change his dressings and that the oncologist would be in to see him as well.

Ernie became progressively worse during the next three weeks. The tumor completely obstructed his flow of bile, and he was becoming very jaundiced. Since he was unable to eat, he was losing weight from his already thin frame. I saw him every other day and became increasingly distressed every time I saw him. I could do nothing to help him. By the sixth week, he was emaciated and more deeply jaundiced. I missed seeing Ernie two nights in a row. I made a point to see him on the third night, after I returned from a project in Philadelphia, regardless of how late it was. I walked into his room around ten o'clock in the evening.

He looked at me with a hurt expression on his face and said, "Where have you been, Doctor?"

I was stricken with guilt. "I have really been busy, Ernie, and just got back from the university. I'm sorry I didn't stop by the last two nights, but it was very late when I got back to Reading."

He looked at me in a way a father would look at an errant son and said, "That may be, Doctor, but I think you know that I am going to die and that there's nothing you can do to help me. This is why you're not coming by to see me anymore. I have to tell you that I really need you now . . . to help me die."

I cannot explain how I felt. My legs gave out, and I collapsed into a chair. I burst into an uncontrollable torrent of tears. All the sorrow and anguish I felt about losing Ernie as a friend and as a patient was expressed in that outpouring of sorrow and grief. I put my head on his bed next to his hand, and I put my hand on his shoulder, and I cried and I cried.

"Ernie, I am so sorry. I am sorry that I did not see you. I'm sorry that I cannot help you."

"But, Doctor," he said, "you can help me now. I really need you to help me. I feel so alone and hopeless in this bed. I need you to be my friend. I am going to need you to help with Molly after I'm gone. She is going to take this very hard. I will need you to help her."

Those few words changed my whole attitude about terminal patients and much of my approach to death and illness. I realized in that instant that my role as a physician for the dying patient was not just to relieve suffering and to try to cure disease but to help people to die. After all, dying was the kind of suffering physicians should be able to relieve. For the first time since Ernie's illness and his hospitalization, I felt like a physician. I knew that I could do something. I could help him to die with dignity and with as little pain as possible.

From then on, I visited him every day, and sometimes twice a day. Often times, Ernie would tell me jokes, and other times, he would ask me to look in on Molly and do this or that for her.

One evening when I arrived, he was sitting up in bed, more like halfway propped up. He seemed eager to speak with me. His thin, jaundiced face lit up, excited. He seemed markedly improved since the night before.

"I'm glad to see you, Doctor. I have something to tell you." There was a certain eagerness in his voice, which seemed slightly stronger than it had been the day before. He beckoned me to come closer to his bed. I pulled up a chair so that I could sit as close as possible.

Ernie looked at me intently. "You remember when you asked me why I thought I was going to die of cancer?"

"Yes, I remember, Ernie. But you really didn't respond to my question then."

"Now I'll answer that question for you," he said. "I have never told this to anybody, and I hope that you do not repeat it to anyone."

"Of course not," I was quick to reassure him.

"About three years ago, I was sitting on my porch, looking at the sun going down, thinking about what I was going to do the next day, when I thought I heard Molly calling me. I went over to the door and said, 'I'm here, Molly.' But she wasn't in the house. So I went back and sat on the chair.

"I thought maybe I was just hearing things, getting old, you know. Then I heard it again. 'Ernie,' someone said. Again, I couldn't find anyone. 'Gee,' I thought, 'I'm hearing things.'

"Then I got a message in my head that said, 'Ernie, it's time to come home.' But I was home. Why would I hear something like that?"

Ernie didn't give me time to answer. He continued telling his story. "Then I heard another message. It said, 'It is time to come home' and 'God loves you.' I was really scared. Chills went up my back, and my hands began to tremble. Just then Molly came out, looked at me, and asked, 'Ernie, are you okay?'

"I told her, 'Sure, I'm okay, Molly. I just had a little chill. I'm okay.'

"I didn't want to tell her what I thought I had heard or what message I thought I received, because she'd think something was wrong with me. So I just let it go and didn't tell anybody. During the next three years, I got some other messages that told me I was going to come down with something bad, something like cancer. The messages never said when I was going to be sick or when I would die, but they always said it would be soon. That is why I was so certain, Doctor, that I had a bad disease when the x-ray was positive."

I listened closely, saying nothing, and let Ernie finish what he was trying to tell me.

"I must tell you this also, and please don't think that I'm crazy. I have had a couple of these messages since I'm in the hospital. They all tell me that there is a future life and that I will be very happy and that I should not worry about Molly. Sometimes I ask questions, but I never seem to get a straight answer. One thing I found is when I hear these voices, I am filled with happiness and everything seems okay. Even the thought of dying gives me a kind of joy. Now I know you might think that this is crazy . . . but you are my friend, as well as my doctor, and I wanted you to know. Please don't tell anyone else about this, because I don't want people to think that I was out of my mind when I died."

"Ernie, I don't think you're crazy," I responded. "I think that you're a wonderful person who has been blessed by God in more ways than one. I appreciate your telling me this, and you can trust that I will tell no one. You must be a very special person. I believe that God has sent an angel to talk to you. Do you realize how very few times in recorded history that this has happened?"

"Oh, Doctor," Ernie protested. I knew his innate humility would not allow him to accept what I had said. "I'm not a special person. I am just an old Dutchman."

We sat together in silence for a moment as I processed what Ernie had told me. He turned his face toward me. He leaned closer, ever so slightly, and spoke again, more quietly than before.

"Doctor . . . can you hear me? I have something else to tell you, something that will really sound insane. I don't understand what I actually heard, or what I think I heard, but he said the same words to me three times right before I went to sleep. I would hear the voice just when I started to fall asleep, and I thought I was dreaming. One time I was wide awake. It was no dream. I just wonder . . . can you hear me and understand what I'm saying?"

I assured Ernie that I heard him very clearly and understood what he was saying, and he continued.

"Two nights ago, before I fell asleep, the voice said something that I did not understand at all. I'm going to try and repeat what I thought he said . . . it sounded something like this: 'Rake the weeds and the cats in the turnip patch and eat them.'" Ernie took a breath and shook his head slightly. "Now you and I both know that doesn't make any sense, but he said it twice and I think a third time, right before I fell asleep. Does that make any sense to you, Doctor?"

I thought about it for a moment. It surely did not make any sense to me. I told Ernie that I was not good at interpreting dreams. He said he did not want me to interpret it. He just wondered if the words made any sense, or was he really going crazy? I assured him he was not going crazy. I remained by his bed. As we talked about other things, I kept turning his phrase over in my head.

All of a sudden, I knew what the phrase was. The words came into my mind from a long time ago, a deeply imbedded memory from my days in a Catholic seminary. Our lessons and all the Masses were in Latin. The realization hit me that the voice was speaking in Latin. "Ernie. What the voice said . . . did it sound something like this: *Requiescat in pace in eternum?*"

"Doctor!" he exclaimed, "I think that's exactly what he said! Please say that again and a little slower, because I'm sure those are the words."

Again, I repeated the Latin, *"Requiescat in pace in eternum."*

"That's it!" Ernie said loudly. "That's it, that's it! What does that mean, Doctor? You seem to understand what he said. Is this some kind of foreign language or something?"

I was overcome. I silently translated from the Latin that was my second language.

Rest in eternal peace.

"Yes, Ernie, it is a foreign language, and it is a religious saying." I didn't tell him the exact translation. "That was an angel, Ernie, telling you to have a good night's sleep. Essentially, he said to rest well."

The relief was evident, and Ernie was in a state of what I can only describe as wonder. "Well, I'll be, ain't that just something? I'll have to tell Molly about that, even if she thinks I'm crazy . . . but Doctor, now I don't think she will."

A quiet contentment settled over Ernie's face. He was ready to sleep. I closed the door to his room and headed out of the hospital to go home.

I left Ernie that night fully realizing how little I knew about God and his creatures. With Ernie, I was in the presence of a very special person. He may have been a simple citizen in the eyes of the world, but God had chosen to show special favor to my friend Ernie. I was spellbound with wonder, for I was privileged to know someone who had actually been spoken to by an angel, someone God the Almighty had favored. I was struck by the majesty of God, how profoundly he cared for all of his creatures. I was deeply humbled by the revelation and wondered why I had been given the privilege to know about it.

I felt a need to stop the car before I got home to my waiting family. I pulled off the road at the Reading Airport, to contemplate all that had happened that night. Ernie knew not one word of Latin and was not a Catholic. I remember being frightened for a brief moment, that disturbing unease in the face of something unknown, a curious kind of fear mixed with awe.

As I looked up at the sky filled with stars, closer and brighter than I had ever seen them, that fear gave way to a feeling of great majesty. I was wonder-struck with the immensity of the universe and filled with belief. I realized fully that God is with each and every one of us. How could we so often squander our days mindlessly unaware, doing so many unkind, Godless things to each other?

I was eager to get home and tell my wife Joanne all about what had happened, even though I didn't know how she would take my story of translating an angelic message from a dying patient. When I turned into our lane and saw the lights of our home, an indescribable feeling settled over me. I felt an understanding deep within my heart that within the angelic phrase of comfort to my dying patient and friend, that there was a message for me too, about life, death, and the certainty of God's love.

In the visits that followed, I learned much from Ernie about life, medicine, being a doctor, what it means to be a friend, life hereafter, facing death and the agony of dying, and the joyful release of surrendering to God's will. From that little dying Dutchman, I got more insight into the meaning of life and death than from all the formal education and all the books that I had read in medicine and philosophy.

I was standing by Ernie's bed late one night as his fragile body was shutting down. He put his thin, feeble hand on mine and said to me in a whisper, "The next time we see each other, my friend, things will be better." I lowered myself into the chair close to the bed.

"Yes, Ernie," I said, "I believe they will."

My eyes welled with tears. I placed my head on his bed so that he could not see how broken up I was. He put his frail hand on my shoulder and gave me a few gentle pats. He said nothing, for we both knew what we were feeling. A few hours later, he became comatose and remained unconscious until he drew his last breath two days later.

My friend Ernie had a very special insight. By sharing in Ernie's experience of death, I had received a message of hope and healing. The spiritual impact of this special gift influenced my perception and awareness, both as a doctor and as a human being, throughout the rest of my life.

CHAPTER 4

A Calling

My path to becoming a physician was long and circuitous. It began with my childhood desire to become a priest. But four years into the seminary, spiritual doubts and questions led me to reconsider my plans. While I was working through that, a world war broke out. And then I fell in love. But I will start at the beginning.

You could hear the trains go by both night and day and listen to the whistle play its single, dying note as it rushed headlong into the darkness. As a child, I never knew where these trains originated, or where they were going. I never thought to question an adult about them. Later, I found the tracks were part of the Reading Railroad system, which served Philadelphia, New Jersey, Delaware, and Maryland. We lived in the city of Reading, about five hundred yards from the Schuylkill River. Our house was less than one hundred yards from the railroad tracks, and passing trains were a part of life.

I was born in that house on a cold winter day at 1:30 a.m. on January 27, 1926. Since I was a big baby, ten and a half pounds, the general practitioner, Dr. Leland Way, delivered me with low outlet forceps, as my father administered open-drop ether to my mother. He placed one drop at a time onto a gauze face mask she wore. This home-delivery relief was used to bring in many a child in the 1920s.

My family lived in a tight-knit community. My father was the son of Italian immigrants. Our street had only five houses, all owned by my grandfather, and all occupied by our relatives. Since my mother was of English and Welsh descent, we did not speak Italian in our home. The third child of six, I had four brothers and a sister.

When I was five and a half years old, my mother was diagnosed with tuberculosis and was sent to the tuberculosis sanatorium, a country estate in the wooded western part of the county, for eighteen months. In those days, a sanatorium was a safe environment for patients with highly contagious TB, not to be confused with the later facility, called a "sanitarium" for the mentally ill.

The six of us children were farmed out to relatives. The younger ones stayed on the same street with my dad's relatives. Two of my brothers and I were sent to live in Delaware with my mother's relatives, Uncle Howard and Aunt Lorena, who lived on a farm without central heat, running water, or an indoor bathroom. We went to a one-room country school. Each of the eight grades was represented by one row of desks and taught by a single teacher, Miss Moore. She was short and stocky with gray hair and gold-rimmed glasses. She spent time with each row during the day, teaching each grade a lesson and giving an assignment. There were only two of us in first grade, and we got a lot of attention. Most of the time Miss Moore taught the four younger grades in the morning, and after lunch, we would look at books or color while she taught the older four grades in the afternoon, who were given math assignments or reading to do. When nature called, we had to raise our hands, with one finger or two. On the way out, we had to flip a handmade sign from green to red, to denote that someone was using the outhouse. We spent an entire year in Delaware. I loved being on the farm and would continue to visit whenever I had the opportunity.

When we returned home, we attended parochial school. Ours was essentially an Irish parish. The only exceptions were two Italian families and one Polish. By the time I was in third grade, I was already a veteran scrapper. We had battles with the Irish kids just about every day. If they weren't throwing stones at us, they would form gangs that tried to beat us. Each day produced another conflict.

My problem nun was Sister B., a tall, thin, hatchet-faced, bespectacled woman with long, boney fingers. She punished me two to three days a week by putting me under her desk for most of the morning. She would pull her habit up to her knees and open her legs. This went on for the whole year. I never fully understood why she would put me under the desk. Not until many years later, when I studied psychosexual pathology in medical school, did I realize she had a serious sexual hang-up.

My adventures under the desk were accompanied by periodic beatings. Sometimes she would slap me. Other times she whacked the end of my fingertips with a sixteen-inch ruler. She would spell my name and deliver a blow of the ruler with each letter. Punishment for Irish students was different. They would receive three blows, representing the first letters of their names.

Sister B. taught third grade and fourth grade. When she did not pass me to fourth grade, I had to repeat third grade. I did not understand why I was kept back, because I could read better and spell better and answer more catechetical questions than any other student in the third grade. My brother Joe was in the fourth grade, and she held him back as well. The following year, I was promoted to fourth grade, but the beatings continued.

Joe was beaten so badly that my father decided to take us out of parochial school.

We were enrolled in Riverside public school. The day we were to change schools, my mother and father arrived to pick us up. I was gathering my few possessions from my desk when Sister B. approached me, put her arm around my shoulder, and looked at me. My first thought was that she was going to strangle me, but instead, she looked at me with sorrow and said, "Peter, I have done you a grave injustice. I hope that when you're old enough to understand, you will find it in your heart to forgive me."

She said good-bye and that was the last time I ever saw her. I did forgive her and prayed for her, for she certainly was a tortured human being. Most likely she became a nun because of the terrible economic situation in Ireland. Many young girls were forced into convents for one reason or another. Sister B. had a definite sadistic tendency, but I think her life must have been truly miserable. I cannot remember a single day that she ever smiled.

When my mother became ill again, we were farmed out to relatives once more. I was sent to live with my Aunt Alice and Uncle Joe, my father's brother and sister, in Philadelphia. Uncle Joe served as a priest for a large Catholic parish in the Italian section of the city. He lived in the rectory, which was a very large house. His sister Alice, unmarried and a licensed practical nurse, served as his personal assistant, cook, and housekeeper. This was the first time in my life I had my own room, new clothing all my own, and was an only child. All the priests and nuns were very friendly to me. The church became my second home. I was never forced to go to Mass during the week, but on Sunday, I sat with the altar boys dressed in a cassock and surplice. Something about the atmosphere of the church and the priesthood strongly attracted me. I mentioned to my aunt that I would like to be a priest when I grew up.

The family welcomed the idea of my becoming a priest. My grandmother and my father were extremely happy to hear I was considering the priesthood. As soon as I was old enough, I became an altar boy and spent many hours working in the church with the priest. I did an apprenticeship as a "red cassock." Before I was able to serve Mass as an altar boy, I had to learn all the requisite Latin responses. I was expected to attend all the high Masses, said in Latin, and special services when Catholics observe Holy Days of Obligation. The church became part of my being.

Father Murphy, of our home parish, was an exceptional priest, and in my estimation a very holy man. I remember he encouraged me to pray for "vocation." It was the first time I heard that word. He explained to me that all priests were called by God to the priesthood. Father O'Donnell, our pastor, was sympathetic to my desire, but urged me to attend Catholic high school in ninth grade.

When I enrolled in Catholic high school, I told the nuns at Reading Catholic that I was interested in the priesthood. In contrast to the cruelty of the grade school nuns, these teachers encouraged me in every way to prepare for religious life. They gave me many classic books to read and helped me to study for the entrance examination to the seminary. Admission was highly competitive. My uncle Joe had graduated with high honors from St. Charles Seminary in Philadelphia. Father O'Donnell spent several days helping me to get ready for the test. More than two hundred students took the entrance examination at St. Charles Seminary when I did. The number may have been so high because seminarians were exempt from the draft. Though I did not make it into St. Charles Seminary, Sister Mary Margaret Alacoque suggested a seminary in Little Rock, Arkansas, instead.

I left Reading Catholic in tenth grade to enter St. John's Home Missions Seminary in Little Rock. The challenge of understanding philosophy and theology and the great task of transforming myself from a lover of creature comforts to a servant of God was daunting. Though we were not allowed to form friendships of any kind in the seminary, I never felt alone. A seminarian is there to learn to be forged into a priest. Forging requires heat and pressure, pressure from the pounding hammer of discipline to shape and temper us. We were soon to find that it took strong men or women to travel the spiritual pathway. The result for those seminarians who had the fortitude is a remarkable personal transformation into a man or woman of God. Every type of person comes to the seminary, but only about 30 percent end up as priests.

I thought I had a calling to the priesthood, a vocation, but only God knows who will become a priest.

I had many memorable experiences in the seminary, experiences that left deep impressions on my character and shaped my future life. I loved the academic and spiritual atmosphere, the association with brilliant and holy men, and the closeness to God that I felt so often there. The spiritual nature of a religious life is difficult to describe. The joy, happiness, and satisfaction associated with this life can only be understood by those who feel they are called by Christ to devote their lives to their fellow man as a member of the clergy. Seminary days were exciting, filled with discovery, mystery, and ecstasy. Every day brought a new challenge.

My faith in God was strengthened in the seminary. I am as certain of the existence of God as any human being can be. I grew to understand that as the final goal of creation, we were created by God to be with him. I know that God is merciful and loves us more than we possibly can comprehend.

While studying philosophy, I began to have misgivings about my vocation. I had periods of what is known as spiritual dryness, which is just another name for depression approaching despair. For me, that time was truly the dark night of the soul. Struggling to determine whether or not I had a vocation, I prayed earnestly for guidance. I spoke to my spiritual director and to many of the other faculty members for help in making a decision. When I left in the summer of 1946, I was not certain if I was leaving the seminary permanently. I needed time to make a decision. As I walked out the main gate to take the trolley car to the train station in Little Rock, my mind was filled with a verse from the gospel of St. Luke:

> But Jesus said to him, "No one, having put his hand to the plow, and looking back, is fit for the kingdom of God." (Luke 9:62)

I understood this verse to mean that anyone who followed Christ should never look back, nor doubt for a moment that he was called to serve Christ. This verse has haunted me all of my life. I feared I would not go to heaven if I left the seminary. I questioned my vocation. Was I just unwilling to take on the hard life of a priest? Was I turning my back on God, refusing to answer his call?

Despite my deep faith, I became aware during the fourth academic year that I had serious questions about Catholic doctrine. I wrestled with the concept of original sin. The more I struggled with it, the further I got from wanting to be a priest. During that summer, I realized I could not return to the seminary as long as I was plagued by these doubts. I told Father James Nugent at the seminary that I would like a leave of absence for two years to consider these questions, which he agreed to do.

I told my father of my decision to leave the seminary. He was furious with me. My grandmother never spoke to me again, and my uncle Joe the priest was upset with me. Basically, I was a pariah. What to do? The next day, I enlisted in the Marine Corps.

My four brothers were all in the military during the war. In 1946, the war was not yet officially declared over, so I decided to enlist. My oldest brother Harry was a career Marine, and I always admired him, so I selected the Marine Corp to serve my military time.

After my examination at the Marine recruiting office, I was on my way to Paris Island and boot camp the following day.

CHAPTER 5

Obstacles and Miracles

I found myself at a turning point in my life. I had already learned that events that seemed disastrous to me, like being persecuted by Sister B., and not getting into St. Charles seminary, ended up being revealed as blessings. My entire life had been a series of disappointments, frustrations, and detours from the path I expected to take, but later, I was exposed to rich opportunities I could not have imagined. I joined the Marine Corps to fulfill my civic duties and put some distance between me and my disappointed family.

I had no idea what to expect as a Marine. Hostilities were declared over, but a state of war still existed. There was little chance of my being in combat, but I had no idea what else could happen. I disliked military life; constantly training to kill other humans did not sit well with me. Nevertheless, I admired career military people because of their devotion to their country and their willingness to throw themselves on the sword whenever required.

Of all the things that happened in the Marine Corps, my life took on real meaning and purpose when I met the most beautiful girl in the world, and for the first time, I experienced and understood the meaning of love.

Every Marine can tell you the horrors of boot camp. It is true that some of us really wanted to kill our drill instructor. We were kicked, slapped, punched, yelled at, beaten on the face with a Lanier, and made to feel about as valuable as a piece of street dung. By the time we finished boot camp, we ended up proud to be a Marine and willing to defend our DI, Drill Instructor, to the death. Marines in particular appreciate *esprit de corps.*

I was not a line Marine. I had scored sufficiently high at the rifle range to qualify for sniper school for training as a rifle coach and sniper. As far as I was concerned, a sniper had only one function—to kill. I prayed for a way out. The opportunity came when there was a vacancy for a librarian at the local Marine service club. Although I was well-qualified, and the only one in the battalion who was twenty-one years old, not a noncommissioned officer, and possessed experience in a library, it was almost impossible for me to get out of sniper school. We were down to fewer than twenty-five candidates out of more than two hundred who had started.

Three days after the job announcement, it was clear that no one was able to meet the criteria for the librarian but me. The commanding officer relented and released me from the sniper school. From then on, except for a three-month ocean tour courtesy of the Marine Corps, I never had another rifle in my hands. I was able to continue my education, taking many correspondence courses and reading volumes of books. I was as close to a bibliophile's heaven as I could get, but even better things were in store for me.

During my time in the Marine Corps, I met my future wife, Joanne Elizabeth Rhode, at a USO function. Philip Noll, one of my closest friends in the Marines, was a history buff, who loved to visit historical places in the South. On one occasion, he signed us both up for a tour of Orton Plantation, located just outside of Wilmington, North Carolina. It happened that my buddy Phil was assigned to KP, Kitchen Police, a euphemism for all the messy side jobs in the cafeteria supporting the cooks, the same morning we were supposed to go on our tour. KP took precedence over everything, including guard duty, so I had to take the trip alone. Those of us leaving base boarded a Marine bus in Camp Lejeune and were taken to a staging area in Wilmington where the USO buses and hostesses were waiting for us. It was mid-March, and the azaleas were in bloom.

After leaving the Marine bus, I walked over to the staging area to board a second bus to Orton Plantation. Standing at the door of one bus was the most beautiful girl I had ever seen, a tall, slim, blue-eyed beauty who was smiling as servicemen entered the bus. Something urged me to make a bold statement. "Why don't you get on this bus?" I asked.

"Okay," she said, "I will!"

She stepped onto the bus, and I moved forward to follow her, when I felt a heavy hand on my shoulder and I heard a familiar voice saying, "Puggy! Puggy! How the hell are you?"

It was a friend from boot camp. I turned to him and said, "I'll see you later. Right now, I have to get on this bus." He protested, but I struggled free and moved quickly into the bus to look for my beautiful girl. I thought surely some idiot Marine would be sitting with her and that I had lost my opportunity. With my undying thanks to God, she was sitting alone. I asked her if I could join her.

"Yes," she said, "please do."

I had not the tiniest inkling of what to do in the presence of this girl. All I knew was that she was extremely beautiful, very soft-spoken, and extraordinarily kind and considerate. I was so enthralled that I was lost for words as I sat there beside her. I had pitifully limited experience with girls. She sensed my difficulty and came to my rescue. She started the conversation by asking me where I was from and what I did before I joined the Marines. When I explained that I was from Pennsylvania, her eyes lit up. She told me that she was from Ohio, our Western border state. I asked her how she got to North Carolina. Before we knew it, the buses set out for Orton Plantation. As far as I was aware, we could have been going to the moon. I can remember absolutely nothing of my first visit to Orton Plantation.

After the tour, we returned to the USO, where we enjoyed a light supper. I asked her if she would like to go to a movie. She absolutely loved movies. We went to see *The Egg and I*, which starred Fred McMurray and Claudette Colbert.

Joanne explained to me that she was currently dating a paratrooper from Fort Bragg, North Carolina, and that they planned to get engaged. I told her that he was a lucky guy and wished her all the happiness in the world.

Though I saw her once or twice afterward at the USO dances, I did not spend any time with her again until she graduated from high school. Her family invited me to the ceremony, because her fiancé-to-be could not attend. Immediately after graduation, her family left for Fremont, Ohio, where her mother had purchased a house. I said good-bye to her that evening, thinking I would never see Joanne Rhode again.

Back at the base, most of my time was spent in the library. I had no interest in dating or leaving the post. I had become very interested in studying medicine. Before I left the seminary, I had spoken to Dr. Merle DeWire, my family doctor, about the possibility of studying medicine. I expressed my reservation that I might not be intelligent enough to be a doctor. He looked at me with a very serious expression, but with a smile on his face, and said, matter-of-factly, "Son, anyone who can read Cicero like a native, and Virgil's *Aeneid* line for line, is surely smart enough to be a doctor."

I was surprised to receive a letter from Joanne. I had not heard from her for many months. Opening it, I did not know what to expect. She wrote to tell me that she was no longer engaged and that she was moving back to Wilmington, North Carolina, with her family. She wanted to see me again. I was ecstatic. We made a date to meet at the USO.

I shall never forget seeing her come up the sidewalk approaching the USO. She was absolutely gorgeous! I took her hand and held it in my grip as if I never wanted to let go. She was delighted to see me, too, and the excitement in her sparkling eyes made me feel that this time she was really my girl. We had a wonderful evening. I could hardly wait to see her again.

At every opportunity, I would leave camp to visit her. Our relationship continued to grow stronger. When I was finally discharged in 1948, her mother offered to drive me home to Pennsylvania. This gave our families a chance to meet and spend a day together. I told Joanne that I would write to her. She understood that I would be starting college in a month and would have little free time.

I had been accepted as a premedical student at Franklin and Marshall College in Lancaster, Pennsylvania, my first step toward a medical degree. I began college as a freshman, because my seminary credits had not yet been accepted. We had more than 250 premeds that year at Franklin and Marshall.

At the end of October, Joanne's mother called my mother to say that Joanne wanted to move to Lancaster. Mrs. Rhode explained to my mother that Joanne missed me terribly and that she loved me and wanted to be with me. She did not in any way wish to impose herself on us. She planned to get a separate place to live and work. She just wanted to be close to me. My mother invited Joanne to stay with us.

I was concerned about the move to Lancaster. Joanne's presence would be a distraction from my studies. I was firmly committed to being a physician. I loved Joanne, but I was not ready for a closer relationship. I explained to her that I would not have a lot of time to spend with her in the evenings, because I had to put in at least four hours or more of study. She understood that.

Joanne arrived a week later, and my mother made her feel at home. Since we had no extra bedrooms, Joanne had to sleep on the sofa in the living room. I offered to take the sofa so that she could have my bedroom. She would have no part of that. My books and all of my school things were in my room. She would not hear of disrupting my studies. The morning after she arrived, she went to look for a job and found one at Hamilton Watch. Her job was to place numbers on the face of the dial. When I returned from class that evening, she was beaming to let me know that she would be working and earning money.

Even though we lived in the same house, we saw each other mostly on the weekends. Since she worked second shift, I never saw her at dinner during the week. On Saturday afternoon, we would go out in the country on my motorcycle, a flathead Harley 80, and look for wildflowers to classify. I was taking an extracurricular course in botany to earn a few extra credits. I found the wild flowers and classified them, and Joanne would draw and paint them.

As Christmas approached, Joanne was still living with us. My mother was concerned that the neighbors would talk about a single girl staying at our house, especially because we were not engaged. I had to make a decision. I loved Joanne very much, but I could not afford a wife at that time. I worried about studying, working a job, and being married at the same time. The alternative was to give up Joanne, which I could not face. I asked Joanne to marry me, and she happily said yes. Her Christmas present would be an engagement ring.

My dad and I went shopping for the ring. I was working part-time at the hospital as an orderly. I was making less than $50 a month. My dad knew a jeweler in Reading willing to extend credit to us. We drove there one Saturday to buy the ring. I chose a small diamond that cost 125 dollars. I paid Mr. Kagan, the jeweler, ten dollars down and promised to pay him ten dollars a month. My father said he would guarantee the payments. Mr. Kagan said that was not necessary and that he would trust me. He explained that his son was a doctor. He knew what it cost to go through medical school.

A few days before Christmas, I planned a treasure hunt so that Joanne would have to search for her ring. It was a sheer delight to watch her following the clues, going from one place to another. Her excitement built as she realized she was getting closer to her goal. When she finally found the ring, she showed such happiness and delight. It was as if she had found the greatest treasure in the world, even though the diamond was miniscule. Years later, when we could well afford an expensive diamond, she refused to consider a gift of a new ring. She loved her little diamond. There were so many wonderful things about her, but this was especially important to me. Her attachment to our engagement ring told me she loved me for myself, not what I could be, or was going to be, or what I had. She was the dearest woman in the world.

When spring arrived, Joanne was completely absorbed in preparing for our wedding. I, on the other hand, was becoming more and more disturbed. The priesthood was firmly entrenched in my mind. It was not so much that I wanted to be a priest, as it was the guilt of turning my back on God. So what if I did not *want* to be a priest? If I had a calling, then, that was my duty, I reasoned, and I needed to shoulder the cross and carry it wherever the Lord led me.

My love for Joanne would rise in my mind and conflict with these thoughts. The torment at times was unbearable, for once married, I could never return to the seminary. I would have made an irreversible choice. I would have shut God out of my life.

The idea of hurting Joanne was killing me, but the thought of eternal damnation for rejecting God was even more painful and horrifying. Day by day, the conflict grew within me as we approached the wedding date. A crisis was pending.

In the middle of April, the crisis hit hard. I would be married in two months and could never return to the seminary. My conscience tormented me night and day. I found it difficult to concentrate on my studies. I had difficulty eating and sleeping. Joanne knew something was wrong, but every time she asked me what was going on, I said everything was fine.

One Saturday afternoon, she came into my bedroom where I was studying. She looked at me very seriously and asked, "Peter, do you want to go through with this marriage, honestly?"

I burst into tears. I went over and hugged her. I was so shaken I could not speak.

"You are not certain about giving up the priesthood, are you?" she asked with tears welling in her clear blue eyes.

"Oh, honey," I cried, "please forgive me! I am so terribly distraught. I'm worried that if I marry, I have turned my back on God."

She hugged me and then nodded her head, indicating that she understood I could not marry her. She said she would leave for home the next day. To this day I feel the anguish of knowing I caused her exceedingly great pain.

I do not remember what happened during the weeks after Joanne left. Somehow, I managed to get through the school year successfully.

In the end, I was thinking about Joanne more than I was thinking about going back to the seminary. I realized I should forget the seminary and marry her. I knew how Caesar felt when he crossed the Rubicon. I jumped on my motorcycle and sped away to the telegraph office. I sent a brief note: "Love you, want to come down and discuss marriage. Peter."

Two hours later, a telegram arrived. "Come down. Will discuss terms of surrender. Love, Joanne."

We had a very simple wedding with just a few guests on July 2, 1949, in the rectory of the church. After a wedding dinner at home, Joanne and I took off for a one-night honeymoon in Washington, DC. Since we had only thirteen dollars, we had a sparse supper at the hotel. Our love for each other made up for everything else. I have never forgiven myself for not having the resources to treat her like a queen and to give her every comfort possible. She never complained once in all our marriage together about the wedding or the one-night honeymoon.

As we were driving home from Washington, I was extremely happy. At this point in my life, I considered, I had just about everything that a young man could ask for: I had a beautiful, wonderful wife and a family who supported me in my desire to become a physician, I was in an excellent premed college, and I was doing well in my studies. Fate, however, would change all this, and it would happen soon.

Sometime in the fall after I returned to school, Joanne found out she was pregnant. She had problems and the doctor prescribed bed rest for her. Six months into the pregnancy, on

Valentine's Day, she went into labor and delivered prematurely. We named the baby Paula Louise. The pediatrician informed me that it did not look good. Our baby daughter was becoming progressively jaundiced. Medical technology had not yet advanced to the treatments provided for today's premature babies. Our tiny girl lived only three days. I held my young wife as I told her I baptized Paula before she died. Joanne's recovery took a long time.

By late spring, Joanne was feeling better. I felt that we had made it through, all was well, and that we were back on track. Surely, the road ahead was well-paved, smooth, and filled with light. Or so I thought.

In the early summer, my brother, Mark, convinced me to join an active army reserve unit in Lancaster, a tank battalion, with him. The army paid five dollars for every meeting we attended. Five dollars was a lot of money in 1950, so I joined up. Joanne was vigorously opposed to my decision, because she felt there would soon be another war.

"Oh, Joanne, there is nothing to worry about," I reassured her. "Wars only occur every twenty years. There is no possible way we would be in a war now. Besides, I can resign any time I want to."

Sometimes we make bland statements that we want to believe. As a premed student, I was so far removed from the everyday world that I failed to see the coalescing events. Little did I know that a great detour was ahead for us.

It was a very good summer. We took many motorcycle trips and made many new friends. When I returned to school in the fall, I was carrying a heavy load, because I wanted to finish in three years rather than four. The dean gave me enough credit for my seminary courses to qualify me as a senior that year.

On October 5, I was sitting in the hospital cafeteria reading the morning paper right after breakfast. I noticed a small item on the first page. "Local Tank Battalion Called for Active-Duty." To my horror, it was Company C, 318 Tank Battalion, my reserve unit. I raced to the armory to resign. It would be catastrophic to interrupt my premed classes. When I burst into the commanding officer's office, the officer was in full uniform. Captain Reardon was on active duty. When I announced that I wanted to resign my enlistment, he said, "Too late, soldier. You are in the army now. Our unit was activated two days ago, and you will report tomorrow morning for active-duty, in uniform. Your visit this morning will save me having to notify you."

I was crushed.

No matter how well you plan, no matter how rough the road you have traveled, no matter how happy you are, there is always an element of the unknown. Although I have never been a fatalist, experience had shown me that if something bad was going to happen, usually it would be really bad.

I remember a Marine in my platoon who was a real grump, always mad. One day, I asked him, "Beakie, why the hell are you always so pissed off?"

"Puggy," he replied, "I am not always pissed off. I just know that no matter how happy I am in the morning, some son of a bitch is out there waiting to ruin my day. I am just preparing myself for that SOB."

I went to the dean's office to explain my situation. Dr. Breidenstein said I could pick up my studies when I returned.

Camp Polk, Louisiana, where I was stationed, was a deserted World War II camp staffed by very few soldiers until it was opened again for the Korean War. Our battalion was a Tank

Battalion. I was in Company C of that battalion, and we were attached to a group known as the Seventeenth Group, a collection of three armored battalions. Initially I was sent to Fort Knox in Kentucky to train as a tank artillery instructor. While in the military school, I applied for transfer into the medical detachment of our battalion. I was not doing well with the non-commissioned officers (NCOs) in charge of Company C. They hated college men, and I realized they were doing everything they could to send me to Korea.

Again, my prayers were answered, and I was transferred into the medical detachment under the command of a second lieutenant, Lt. Steve Carrington. My life changed dramatically as I no longer had to worry about being sent overseas. Several months later, I was assigned as NCO in charge of the Seventeenth Group Medical Dispensary.

The medical officer in charge, Captain Jordan, trained me to do minor suturing, along with certain diagnostic skills and some basic pharmacology. There was no actual course offered to me, so I supplemented my medical education by reading all the technical books available to me in the dispensary. It was an incredible opportunity to learn, and I picked up many skills during that period.

While working in the dispensary, I came upon a notice announcing a four-month course on medical technology offered at Brooks Army General Hospital in San Antonio, Texas. I realized that with the knowledge I would gain from this premier course, I could finance my way through medical school. I filled out an application and sent it to the commanding officer, a very strict West Point graduate. The application came back with DISAPPROVED written in very large letters on the bottom, signed by Colonel Klaus. I was neither dismayed nor discouraged, knowing that this initial rejection was the usual situation in most battalions. I waited a month, obtained a new application, and sent that in for approval by Colonel Klaus. The next morning, I was summoned to the colonel's office. I knew the colonel was going to rake me over for sending the application again after he had denied it.

No sooner had I walked into the colonel's office, than he started to berate me. When he asked why I wanted to be a medical technologist, I told him that I planned to study medicine and was very interested in medical technology. He replied that not every civilian cook could be an army cook, not every civilian truck driver could be an army truck driver. I said I agreed, but it would be a better army if some of the civilian cooks could be army cooks rather than trying to make cooks out of truck drivers. He was not pleased with my response. He said if I sent that application in again, he would have to take disciplinary action.

I took the application, folded it, and put it in my pocket. I saluted him, did an about face, and left his office. I walked back to the dispensary, dejected about missing a great opportunity. On the way back, I said a special prayer that by some miracle the colonel would change his mind. As I neared the dispensary, I saw the colonel's Jeep on the way to the motor pool for his morning inspection.

The dispensary staff was finishing up the morning sick call, seeing the last few soldiers who were malingering or really sick. As we were cleaning up after surgery, a Jeep screeched to a halt in the parking lot. In came Colonel Klaus, accompanied by a major and a captain.

The colonel's face was badly burned. A large blister hung from the tip of his nose, his eyebrows were singed, and his lips were swollen. We got him on the treatment table, and I gave him a shot of morphine sulfate to ease his pain. Cold compresses were applied to his lips and eyes. I opened the blister on his nose and rearranged the skin and then covered the area with a cold compress.

We got the full story. At the motor pool, Colonel Klaus had asked for a light for his cigarette. A very tall man, about six feet four, he bent over while the attendant warrant officer flicked him a light with a Zippo. The officer had just filled the lighter with high-octane gas. When the spark hit the gasoline-soaked wick, it shot a foot-high flame right into the colonel's face.

A quarter hour after the injection and the treatment, the colonel was feeling much better. He complimented me on my treatment skills. He sat up and asked for cigarette. After lighting up, safely this time, he said, "If there's any way I can return a favor to you, Sergeant, please let me know."

I jerked the paper out of my pocket and said in the most benign voice I could muster, "Would the colonel please reconsider my application and approve it?"

He looked at me and tried to smile, but it was too painful. He grimaced instead.

"Give me that damn application," he replied.

Taking a pen from his pocket, he scratched off DISAPPROVED and replaced it with a bold APPROVED. He re-signed the form, dated it, and noted the time. Once again, a last-minute reversal of fortune turned an obstacle into a miracle. Within hours, Joanne and I were on our way to San Antonio, two happy kids if ever there were.

Toward the end of my duty, we were delighted to find that Joanne was pregnant. We were beyond happy, because prenatal care at Brooks Army General was absolutely the best anywhere in the world. I felt secure that all would go well this time.

Our reserve unit was notified that we would be discharged within ten days. Joanne and I were overjoyed. We were eager to return to our academic studies and our home. After two years in the army, we were able to secure all of our possessions on the roof of a small 1941 Pontiac coupe we had purchased. Once that precious discharge paper and mustering-out pay were in my hands, we headed our car west by northwest, home to Pennsylvania.

We stopped over in Arkansas. I wanted to show Joanne the seminary. She was anxious to see it after all she had heard about my time there. We walked around the grounds and visited the grotto I had worked on for more than two years. When we entered the Prep building, she said she could actually see me as a seminarian walking the halls.

Once settled in an apartment in Lancaster, I contacted Dr. Breidenstein at Franklin and Marshall to arrange my schedule for the next year. I went to see the superintendent of St. Joseph's Hospital where I had worked as an orderly before going into the army. I spoke with the head nun, Sister Saint Kevin, and told her since my training as a medical NCO and my studies in San Antonio, I was trained as a medical laboratory technician, as an emergency medical technician, and that I had essential nursing skills. She looked at me and said, "Peter, you have certainly come a long way since I last saw you. I would like you to take the position of night nurse in the emergency ward. In addition, you could serve as emergency laboratory technician, if time allows. Do you think you can handle that position?"

I replied without hesitation, "Absolutely, Sister!"

I started that night as the nurse in the emergency ward.

Around mid-November, the dean of the School of Medicine of the University of Pennsylvania visited our campus. This was the first and only time Dr. John Mitchell ever visited Franklin and Marshall. Most of the smaller college visits were made by the assistant dean, or one of the other professors. I felt very privileged when the dean of our college called me to be interviewed by Dr. Mitchell. The interviews were held in Dr. Breidenstein's office.

The premedical students were called one at a time. Until your turn, you waited in the small area outside of the dean's office. We were told that the interview was equally as important to getting into medical school as our grades. If the interviewer either did not like you, for any reason, or did not think you were material to turn into a doctor, you were dead in the water. This created a great deal of stress with most students, because it was an all-or-nothing proposition. Strangely, I was not one bit nervous. Having been ripped apart by drill instructors, sergeants, and officers, criticized and evaluated, humiliated and honored, ridiculed and praised, I was ready for anything. We were told that Dr. Mitchell was one of the most outstanding medical school deans.

Dr. John Mitchell was an internationally known pediatrician, who had served as dean of the medical school for several years. Not only was he an extremely kind and practical person, but he was also genuinely interested in medical students. He considered the most essential characteristic of a medical student, beyond basic intelligence, to be integrity. He felt strongly that honor was a *sine qua non* characteristic, that is, an absolutely essential part of a physician. When I entered the room, Dr. Mitchell rose to greet me, shook my hand, and asked me to sit in a chair in front of him. I estimated he was between fifty-five and sixty years old. He had a very disarming, friendly demeanor, and his bearing was one of exceptional confidence. Dr. Mitchell first put me at ease and asked me, along with some questions about my background, why I wanted to be a physician. The first thing out of my mouth was, "I think I'd really enjoy being a doctor."

I told him about my background, that I studied first to be a priest, was in the Marine Corps and the army, was married with a baby son, and that we had lost a child. I was determined to become a physician. He seemed to keep me considerably longer than he did the other interviewees. Many of his questions were personal, very little about my finances or academic record. Of course, he had all this information from the dean's office. After I answered all his questions, he said, "Peter, we will definitely consider you for the class of 1954."

I was very happy to hear this, but I replied, "Dr. Mitchell, I am actually applying for 1953. I have already lost so many years in the service that I would really like to apply for 1953."

"Peter," he responded, "the class of 1953 has long been chosen. In fact, there is a list of seventy-four alternates. You would be the seventy-fifth alternate."

"I realize those odds are tremendous, Dr. Mitchell," I said, "but I would like to be considered for the class of 1953."

He rose, shook my hand, and, smiling, said, "We'll consider you."

As I left there, I prayed that I should be accepted to the University of Pennsylvania. I did not feel confident against the odds that I faced. I have had a few experiences in my life where the odds were definitely stacked against me, but praying seemed to give me an edge. I kept on working and studying and praying, and I put my trust in God.

The University of Pennsylvania School of Medicine was the oldest medical school in the United States and one of the most prestigious. Being number seventy-five on the list of all alternates did not give me a great deal of confidence that I would be selected for the class of 1953. I began to look around at foreign medical schools because all of the American medical schools had selected the candidates for 1953. I had my choice of either party schools or Swiss schools. After reviewing six of the schools, I found the University of Lausanne in Switzerland had an excellent reputation and that they were still accepting students. The only difficulty that faced me was that all classes were held in French. Though I had taken two years of French, I did not have a speaking knowledge of the language. I applied to Lausanne anyhow and was accepted. A letter arrived in English, stating that I would have to be fluent in French by the fall if I were to enroll. With this in mind, Joanne and I closed our apartment to save enough money for passage to Europe. She moved home with our son, Steven, to live with her mother. I moved into the hospital, in a tiny room in back of the Convent. We were determined that we would overcome every obstacle to my becoming a doctor.

As the months rolled by, I worked in the laboratory of St. Joseph's Hospital in Lancaster and substituted as the backup ambulance driver. Later on, I served as a nurse in Emergency on the eleven to seven night shift.

I was in the hospital blood bank one night, cross-matching some blood for a morning operation when I had a telephone call from Dr. Breidenstein, the dean of Franklin and Marshall. He wanted to know if I was taking any additional credits in English. I told him that I was taking a two-credit course in English poetry. He said that he was very happy to hear that, because I lacked two credits in English in order to qualify for the University of Pennsylvania School of Medicine. He informed me that Dr. Mitchell had just called to let him know that he had placed me on the list with the seventy-four alternates. One young woman had elected to get married rather than to study medicine. I was chosen from the list to fill the one open spot in medical school! I was speechless.

The dean picked up the conversation and said, "Peter, you must send fifty dollars tomorrow morning to the university, along with the papers I have here on my desk, to guarantee your place in the class."

I didn't have fifty dollars. My father was in Chicago and would not return for a few more days. I explained this to the dean, who said that he would pay the fee for me. The dean encouraged me to get down to his office the next day to sign those papers. The intercession by this extraordinary man left me dumbstruck with gratitude. I held the phone in my hand for a few heartbeats, my soul filled with images of the kindness and generosity of so many people who helped me get to this place in my life. This was truly a gift from God.

The first thing I did was to call Joanne and tell her that I was accepted at the University of Pennsylvania and that I would be down to get her during the Easter holiday. We were thrilled that we did not have to go to Switzerland and that I had been accepted to one of the finest medical schools in the world. The next thing I did was to fall on my knees and thank God for this wonderful gift and for all the other blessings he had given us.

Lulled into a sense of security, I thought it would be smooth sailing from this point, with so much disruption behind us. I felt so abundantly lucky, and I believed that it was meant to be and that all things would align in our favor.

A few days before graduation, the dean called me and asked me if I could bring my high school diploma to his office. I told him that I had never gotten a high school diploma. He was shocked. He had certified that I had a diploma when I was accepted at the University of Pennsylvania. He said in order to graduate, I had to have a diploma within the next day. The only place I could possibly get a high school diploma was Reading Catholic High School, which I had attended only to tenth grade. I called the principal, Mother Evangeline, to beg for her help.

After a few respectful pleasantries, I had to explain why I needed her to drop everything and create a high school diploma for me.

"Mother Evangeline," I explained, "I am to graduate from Franklin and Marshall College in two days. I am required to produce my high school diploma to get into medical school!"

She knew that I had completed three years in the seminary and that I certainly qualified for a high school diploma. "Peter," said Mother Evangeline, "I promise to have a diploma ready for you when you get here. You may come right away." I raced to Reading on my motorcycle, went to her office, and there she was with a diploma.

I offered to pay for the documents. Smiling, the gracious nun said there would be no charge. She just wanted me to say a prayer for her and for Father Ring, both of whom had signed my diploma. I was so happy I could have kissed her, but I knew that would not have been a good thing. I thanked Mother Evangeline again profusely and assured her that I would pray for both of them.

The Lord had blessed me again. One by one, the obstacles had been cleared. There was little question now that it was my destiny to be a doctor. Although the spiritual quandary of leaving the priesthood would take me many years to reconcile, the framed documents on my office wall serve as a visual reminder that with God, all things are possible.

My high school diploma is dated June 2, 1953, and my Bachelor of Science degree is dated one day later, June 3, 1953.

CHAPTER 6

The Making of a Physician

The entrance to the School of Medicine of the University of Pennsylvania opens onto a tree-lined walkway on the Penn campus known as Hamilton Walk. It was here I would spend the next four years, being fashioned into a physician. I had arrived at the end of a long and arduous journey. With only a few more steps to go, I would be in medical school. As I ventured up Hamilton Walk for the first time, I thought of the miraculous events that brought me to this point, cascading through my mind in a kaleidoscopic montage. They were brilliant memories, stark realizations of how often an insurmountable obstacle was somehow removed and the pathway was open again. There were a few times when I felt I should give up, but my will to be a physician forced me to keep moving forward. I knew I did not arrive here solely through my own efforts. So many people along the way helped me, encouraged me, and supported me in one way or the other.

Other students were there gathered on the steps, all freshmen, all with eager, expectant faces. Before I entered the medical school doors, I stopped. I said a prayer. I asked God to help me become a doctor whose main interest was the welfare of his patients. Fully aware that doctors have a high capacity to earn money, that desire was never my main reason for entering medical school.

While a premedical student, I had read the life of Sir William Osler, one of the greatest physicians that ever lived. As I walked up the marble steps to the dean's office, I could feel Osler's presence. He was a professor of medicine at Penn for four years. I was familiar with the Osler aphorisms, and in many of his sayings, he stressed the importance of the patient in the education of the physician. I knew it would be several years before I would have the privilege of examining patients. Osler's admonition, "Medicine is learned by the bedside, and not in the classroom," sounded in my ears and was to stay with me for many years to come.

I was well on the road to becoming a physician. Every student who wishes to be a doctor must take the same road. Surely, there are differences in how we get to the end of that path, but I wondered if perhaps I had already had more twists and turns than most.

My father cashed in his life insurance policy to get the money for my first year tuition. It was $2,400, a very large sum in 1953. For the rest of my time in medical school, I no longer needed to worry about tuition. I received scholarships and a loan from a Pennsylvania medical fund.

The first year of medical school is the point of entry into the anatomy dissecting room and the introduction to cadavers. For most of us, this was a routine procedure. Anatomy requires brute memory and constant association of one structure with another. It was very easy to sever a nerve or blood vessel in the process of dissecting, a mistake severely frowned upon by the anatomy professor. Dr. Williams was an extraordinary teacher from the old school, an erudite professional. One day, after we finished dissecting, I ventured into his office to ask him a question. We got along well. I think he took a special interest in me, because I was a veteran of two wars. I was having a particularly difficult time remembering the origins, insertions, and actions of all the muscles in the body. I was convinced that most physicians practicing medicine remembered no more than ten percent of the body muscles with their origins and insertions. I mentioned this to Dr. Williams. He laughed and told me to pay particular attention to the *adductor longus* in the leg. He then added in Latin *Verbum sat sapienti,* which translates "A word to the wise is sufficient." He knew I understood Latin well. It was a common bond between us. On the final anatomy examination, the *adductor longus* was the only muscle for which the origin and insertion was asked. The second year of medical school was extremely exciting. We focused on pathology and pharmacology. I think pharmacology is the most difficult subject to understand and master. We began to see live patients even though we did not touch them. Though you are a medical student, you do not feel like a doctor the first year. As you get into learning about diseases and treatment of diseases during the second year, you gradually begin to think more like a doctor. My interest in medical research grew during this year of study, because it became apparent that there were many more diseases for which we had no treatment than those for which we did.

Every medical student looks forward to the third year of medical school with great anticipation and eagerness. It is the start of the clinical years. This is the first time we would see, touch, and examine real live patients. We were resplendent in our newly purchased white coats, with a shiny stethoscope in one pocket, and a pen-like flashlight, pen and pencil, and a small plastic ruler graduated in both inches and centimeters, in the other pocket. To complete this professional uniform, each student carried a small leather student medical bag that contained a Welch Allyn diagnostic instrument, a little rubber percussion hammer and a tuning fork. Armed and ready, we medical students ventured onto the wards of the University

Hospital prepared to save the world. Little did we realize that our innocence would be shattered by the end of the first day. We did not expect to be urinated and/or vomited on in the pediatric wards and coughed on by phlegmy, contagious patients. We finally had the opportunity to use everything we had learned in the first two years and put it into practice. Now, we had to combine patient history, physical findings, and laboratory results into a clinical impression. Experience, the great teacher and humbling agent, had us by the throat. On the hospital wards, the medical student had the lowest place on the totem pole, below student nurses and orderlies. Third-year medical students were the object of ridicule by most nurses and by the godlike residents.

I decided early in my third year to be a pathologist and specialize in hematology. A small number of university pathology departments had instituted this dual specialty and provided the necessary training. One of these was Presbyterian Hospital in Philadelphia. The pathologist-hematologist in charge of the department was Dr. Philip Custer to whom I had been introduced. He said I should see him at the end of my third year, to discuss the possibility of a residency program.

On the pediatric service, I saw my first hydrocephalic baby. She had the largest human head I have ever seen, almost three feet across from the brow to the occiput, or back of the head. About a year old, she was a little girl with a normal face and body. The pediatrician explained to us that the flow of fluid inside the brain had become obstructed and was not able to be absorbed by the body. As a result, the cranium enlarged to accommodate the fluid. At the same time, the retained fluid was crushing the brain. There was no treatment available. She was to remain in the hospital until she died. I felt horrible and helpless. My desire to enter into medical research became stronger.

After pediatrics, our group went on to study obstetrics and gynecology at Philadelphia General Hospital, also known as

PGH, or Blockley, one of the oldest hospitals, if not the oldest, in the United States. Most of the medical students in Philadelphia had some part of their training at PGH. It was a very large facility with more than one hundred interns. Most of the patients seen at PGH were either city employees and their families or indigent persons.

On the gynecological ward, there were ten examining rooms. The patient would be prepared in one room, her legs opened and put into stirrups and her chart placed on her abdomen. Tracks ran from the preparation room and terminated at the base of a small stool on which sat a medical student. A curtain was pulled back, and the patient was pushed down the track to the waiting medical student. The procedure was first to read the medical history, followed by a gynecological examination, which consisted of a description of the external genitalia, insertion of the vaginal speculum for a visual examination of the cervix, and a manual palpation of the uterus, fallopian tubes, and ovaries. After the student completed his examination, the resident would enter the room and make his or her examination. The student would then describe to the resident what he or she found during his examination.

Obstetrical service was the one thing we were all looking forward to. The very act of delivering a baby seemed synonymous with being a doctor. PGH had an extremely large obstetrical service with somewhere between ten and fifteen delivery rooms. Interns, residents, medical students, obstetrical nurses, and student nurses made up the army of medical attendants.

On a very busy night, my name was called to attend a woman who was obstetrically classified as a *gravida 12, para 11*. That means she had delivered eleven children and was now pregnant for the twelfth time. She was a large, very pleasant African American woman who was progressing without incident. Since she was fully dilated, the intern was about to move her over to delivery, when a nurse called him. They were having a problem in another delivery room and needed his help. He left as we were moving our patient. We transferred her to the delivery table, arranged her in stirrups, and waited for the intern to return.

Fully gowned, masked, and gloved, I stood at the bottom of the table hoping the intern would return before the baby presented. I had seen at least a dozen or more deliveries, but I was never the sole person responsible for conducting the delivery. A chill went up my spine when the patient announced that she thought the baby was coming. She took one look at me and said, "Now, sonny, don't you be nervous. Just stand there, and I'm going to blow this baby right into your hands!"

Sweat broke out on my forehead, clouding my glasses, and my throat suddenly became dry. Normally, the head crowns when the baby is being born, extends, and then the head rotates right or left in order to accommodate the shoulders. The head would go back to normal position, known as restitution, and the rest of the baby would be delivered easily. Suddenly, the woman about to give birth announced, "Har it comes! Har it comes!"

I saw the head pop out, followed by the buttocks. Panicked, I was just able to grab one foot before the infant plunged headlong into the bucket at the foot of the table. I placed the baby on her abdomen while the nurse aspirated fluid from its nose and mouth. A shrill cry told us all was well. I cut and clamped the umbilical cord before placing the baby on the side table for the nurse to clean up. When the placenta cord lengthened, I was able to express the placenta, after which silver nitrate was instilled in the baby's eyes. The mother was very pleased and commented on every procedure. In fact, she actually directed me how to do them. "Now, sonny, you take that there . . ." She was certainly more experienced than I was.

I had delivered my first baby. It was an incredibly proud moment, though in reality, I had just watched the baby being born as nature intended. I felt more like a doctor that day than ever before. That evening at dinner in the hospital cafeteria, all the medical students on obstetrics proudly talked about their deliveries. Little did I know that the reality of obstetrics was about to present itself to me in its most deadly form.

It was a Sunday night. I was up for the next obstetrical patient. She turned out to be a fireman's wife named Jane. She was very pretty and pleasant. This was her first baby, and she was very excited about it. Jane was having a painful, protracted labor, which annoyed the intern in attendance. He was one of the directors of the annual Blockley play, which had been put on by the interns for many years. He was anxious to get back to rehearsal, coming in and out of the labor room to see the progress Jane was making. Finally, she had dilated sufficiently to be moved to the delivery room. All went well with the delivery. She had a beautiful little boy who weighed in at eight and a half pounds. The only thing left to do was to deliver the placenta, but the cord did not lengthen. In his haste to get back to rehearsal, the intern began to pull on the cord. To everyone's horror, the uterus suddenly everted, turned inside out. This is one of the deadliest obstetrical emergencies, because the huge venous vessels can empty the body of blood in a matter of minutes. In a state of panic, the intern ran from the room shouting, "Call Dr. Green! Call Dr. Green!"

Dr. Green, the senior obstetrical resident, was known to be on the floor, but I knew this young woman would be near death before he could arrive. I stood there petrified. The lecture on everted uteri flashed into my head. . . . *Strip off the placenta, place the uterus back into the abdominal cavity, and vigorously massage the fundus with your hand in the uterus* . . . I stepped up to the protruding uterus with blood pouring out of every surface and stripped off the placenta. Then I pushed the uterus back up into the abdomen and placed my other hand on the top of it, massaging as vigorously as I could. The blood ran out of the uterus down my arm to my elbow and splashed on the floor. I prayed as I never prayed in my life that this young woman could be saved. In the meantime, the nurse, recognizing the complication, ordered blood for transfusions. I could feel the uterus begin to contract around my hand, but I did not actually know what to do, whether I should remove my hand. Just about then Dr. Green rushed into the room. He quickly assessed everything. He came over to the table, placed his hand over the uterus to feel its state of contraction, and told me it was okay to remove my hand from inside the uterus. As I did, he inserted his hand in the vagina and continued to massage. By this time, the bleeding had subsided. We set up two pints of blood to transfuse her. In an hour, the emergency was over, her blood pressure was stabilizing, and her color was good. She remained in the hospital a little longer than she had anticipated, but thank God, in his infinite mercy, she had survived. I left PGH feeling much more like a physician than when I entered two months earlier.

The Surgical Services at the University of Pennsylvania was the largest and most successful department in the medical school.

Dr. I. S. Ravdin, the chief of surgery, was an extremely dynamic individual, quick in wit, intolerant of stupidity, and famously short-tempered. He was fiercely competitive and a tireless worker. He had worked his way up, first as the chief resident, ending up on the surgical staff of the University of Pennsylvania. He married the daughter of the chief of surgical service. His wife was a physician who became dean of the medical school during the years of World War II. Dr. Ravdin had worked his way to the highest position attainable in a university department and the highest position in surgery in the United States. He had an international reputation as a renowned gastrointestinal surgeon.

It was always impressive to see Dr. Ravdin on the wards, with his retinue of attendant staff, from the lowly medical student to a full professor of surgery. He was notorious for asking questions that most students could not answer. If you were to use an instrument that carried the inventor's name, you had better know the history of that inventor or you would be humiliated before the crowd in attendance at the time. He liked to ask medical students where this or that instrument came from, when anesthesia first appeared in medicine, or who developed antiseptic surgery.

Forewarned, I was about to enter my first operation with the "chief." The first assistant, Dr. Poplar, was a board-certified surgeon and a full professor of surgery, who gave me some information that turned out to be insufficient. Before going into surgery, I was instructed never to contradict Dr. Ravdin or say anything that would upset him.

The medical student was always placed to the right of Dr. Ravdin in order to have the same view of the operative area as the surgeon while being instructed in the procedure. The position gave the professor an excellent opportunity to quiz the medical student. We were all strategically arranged around the patient. The antiseptic had been applied to the area of the incision, when the professor turned to me and asked, "Peter, what can you tell me about these rubber gloves, who invented them?"

Here was my chance to make a few points. I was an avid reader of medical history. I often went to a quiet corner in the medical history section of the library, sat in an overstuffed chair, and enjoyed my lunch reading medical history. I had read extensively about Dr. William Halstead, who had invented the rubber gloves for his surgical nurse, who happened to be his wife, because she was allergic to the antiseptic she applied prior to surgery. Dr. Ravdin was delighted that I knew this bit of information. I did not stop when I was ahead. I did not know that Dr. Ravdin greatly disliked Dr. William Halstead before I went on to edify what a great surgeon Halstead was and how he practiced meticulous bloodless surgery.

Had he taken one of the instruments and stabbed me in the chest, I would not have been one bit surprised, such was his sudden look of malevolence. I could see only Dr. Ravdin's steely eyes, which glared at me in the split second it took me to realize I had deeply upset him. I could see fury and disapproval distorting his face even through his surgical mask. I did not know that Dr. Ravdin believed in a rapid surgical procedure to keep the patient under anesthesia as short a time as possible. He considered the time wasted producing a bloodless field was detrimental to the patient. I wish I had known that before I crammed my foot in my mouth.

Up to that point, the surgery had gone without incident. The tumor was removed, and we were getting ready to resect the bowel, that is, to sew the two ends together. The ends of the bowel were first united, held together with instruments known as Babcock clamps. The clamps were given to me to hold while the surgeon placed the sutures. The first assistant surgeon, Dr. Poplar, had instructed me in exactly what to do.

"Peter, when Dr. Ravdin says to remove a Babcock, you hand it to me, with the finger grips facing toward me." I was confident that I could perform this simple maneuver. I was mistaken.

I removed the first Babcock and handed it to Dr. Poplar as I was instructed to do. Dr. Ravdin roared, "Peter, stop that foolishness!"

"I'm sorry, sir," I said. I did not know what I did wrong but was terrified to ask him.

In went another stitch. A lump formed in my throat, and my hands developed a slight tremble.

"Okay, Peter, take off that next Babcock," Dr. Ravdin said firmly.

I did and handed it to the first assistant surgeon the same way I had previously.

He shouted, "You do that one more time, and I'm throwing you out! You understand that, Peter?!"

"Yes, sir, I do. I'm sorry." I felt the red heat of humiliation rising up my neck and burning my ears.

The tension in the operating room (OR) was palpable. I could see the strain on everyone's face even through their masks. It was hell. Exactly thirty seconds later, the third stitch was put into the gut, tied, and cut. The Babcock had to be removed.

"Take off that next Babcock," Ravdin snapped at me. As I was handing the Babcock to the first assistant, I could sense Dr. Ravdin had become very tense. He turned his head and looked up at me. His face held mix of inexplicable hurt and explosive anger. The tension around the operating table was so high it was painful. With great trepidation and a trembling hand, I removed the Babcock and handed it to Dr. Poplar. A roar pierced through the tense silence.

"That's it! That's it! Now get out! Get out!"

I gave the rest of the Babcocks to Dr. Poplar and started to walk out of the OR. As I was approaching the door, Dr. Ravdin turned his head and shouted, "You go out there and scrub up and get back in here!"

If I was tense before, it had gotten much worse. I knew the surgical team would be doing absolutely nothing except getting hell from the chief while I was scrubbing. The prescribed time for a scrub-up was ten minutes, not one minute more nor a minute less. I knew that wily guy would be watching the clock to make sure I followed the procedure exactly. It was probably the longest ten minutes I ever spent.

I finished scrubbing and entered the OR, dried my hands on a sterile towel handed to me by the scrub nurse, put on a new gown and gloves, and then cautiously made my way to the operating table. I expected more disaster and humiliation. I felt sorry for the staff surgeons assisting at this operation. They were all good people who did not deserve to be brow-beaten while I was scrubbing up. With the caution of a minesweeper, I entered my place on Dr. Ravdin's right side, received the Babcocks handed to me by the first assistant surgeon, and got ready for the next blast.

To my astonishment, Dr. Ravdin did not seem at all angry. The next stitch went into the bowel and was duly tied and cut. The command came to remove the Babcock . . . surely all hell was to follow. I removed the Babcock exactly the same way I had before and handed it to Dr. Poplar. Dr. Ravdin turned to me and said, "Now, Peter, why did you not do that in the first place? Why do you have to aggravate me? All I can do is to try to teach you. If you will not learn, then it is beyond my control." Utterly mystified, I replied with another apology and a promise to try harder the next time.

The rest of the surgery went very well. He explained to me how the stitch should be placed in the bowel to make sure that it was watertight to avoid leakage of the contents of the bowel. He explained the importance of minimal trauma so scarring would not occur. Scarring can produce adhesions, often a complication of bowel surgery. As soon as the last stitch was placed in the bowel, Dr. Ravdin left the OR to go to another OR for a second surgery. The attending staff surgeons were left to close and dress the wound, write postoperative orders, and prepare the next patient for surgery. No one said a word to me, and I did not ask what I had done wrong. I found out later that I had done nothing wrong. The problem was that Dr. Ravdin was upset with my remark about Dr. Halstead. The mention of Dr. Halstead had opened not just a hornet's nest, but a channel of seething hostility. I couldn't possibly have known that Halstead was an arch rival of Dr. Ravdin. Although the exact nature of their conflict was not clear among their contemporaries, Ravdin's disdain for Halstead was legendary. There was no name I could have praised that would have risen in Ravdin's gorge as severely. He was defending his turf and his honor, blowing off steam. Since I was the culprit, I was the victim.

Shortly before I graduated, Dr. Ravdin called me to his office. To my great surprise, he offered me a residency in surgery. To be invited to train at the University of Pennsylvania and to be offered the position by the chief of surgery himself were honors indeed. I thanked him for his kindness and his consideration and told him I was deeply honored by his asking me. I explained that I was interested in understanding the nature of disease. I had a passion for pathology, what causes disease, rather than how to treat the diseases. I was surprised by his thoughtful comments about my medical career. He said that I would be an excellent clinician and would do very well in surgery, suggesting that I could still continue my interest in research. I thanked him for his acknowledgment, kindness, and consideration. It is very hard to say no to a man of Dr. Ravdin's standing.

When I left his office, I realized I had just closed the door on a great opportunity, one that many medical students would have seized upon immediately. As I walked down the corridor passing the surgical wards, I thought of the endless exhausting, backbreaking hours and humiliation the surgical residents had to endure for a period of five long years. Whatever the future held, I knew I had made the right decision in this instance.

My senior year was a very exciting one. Dr. Francis Wood, the chairman of the Department of Medicine, was a kind, unassuming physician, who instilled confidence by his very presence. Dr. Wood had a group of us students examine the same patient, suggest some diagnostic tests, give our clinical impression, and then suggest a course of treatment. On that particular day, the patient was an eighty-year-old female who was having signs of cerebral insufficiency. After we had all examined her and worked out our various diagnoses, Dr. Wood brought us into the small conference room to discuss our findings. When he came to the diagnostic procedures, most of us had suggested arteriograms, perhaps a pneumoencephalogram, and then one or two other rather arduous and painful tests. Dr. Wood then lowered his glasses to the end of his nose, looked over them, straight at us, and said, "Suppose this woman was your mother, or grandmother, what would you do?"

Somewhat startled, we said that we would do none of those awful tests, but limit our test to the smallest number of painless procedures. When he asked why, we responded that those procedures are painful and most likely would not produce any information that we did not already know. We would not want our beloved relative to experience the pain and discomfort of those tests.

Dr. Wood said softly, "Do you not realize this lady is someone's wife or mother or grandmother? As a physician, you must treat every patient as though that patient was your mother or your wife or sister or brother or father. You must ask yourself when you have the responsibility for a patient, 'If I were the patient, would I want me for the doctor?' If you cannot answer yes, you are morally obligated to refer that patient."

The class was dumbstruck. We had never heard this sentiment expressed by any other physician in the past three years. I recognized this advice was the single most important key to practicing good medicine. In years to come, it would be my guiding principle. Dr. Wood changed my outlook on medical practice. We may not be able to cure disease, but we could help the patient to survive it without unnecessary pain.

I had applied for a job as a student physician at the University Student Health Center. There were four seniors selected each year to operate the clinic from six in the evening until seven o'clock the next morning. These positions traditionally went to four student applicants who had obtained the highest scholastic records during the last three years. I was delighted when I was among the students selected.

We were told by the director of the Student Health Center that we should expect an influx of coeds the evening before an examination. There would be so many that it would be difficult to screen them. He offered a suggestion to deal with the problem. He recommended that a coed who appeared with makeup and combed hair should not be seen. He believed that a woman who was really sick would not waste time thinking about how she looks. He was spot on. One evening, when I was on duty, two girls came to the clinic together. One had a severe laceration on her upper leg. My intake interview revealed that the other girl had been shaving her legs with a double-edge razor in the bathroom. She opened the razor to clean it and was shaking it out. The razor struck her friend on the thigh, cutting a four-inch gash. It would be an easy thing to repair.

The deep razor wound contaminated with hair required tetanus antitoxin. She was not aware of being allergic to anything, but I skin tested her first anyway. While I was preparing the suture materials, I heard a thump and turned to see her on the floor, rapidly turning blue. She had an anaphylactoid reaction to the test shot.

Emergency drugs were locked into a cabinet on the wall, and I did not have the key. Only the resident was allowed to administer emergency drugs. I instructed the injured girl's friend to call the hospital operator to ask for a resident to come to the Student Health Center immediately as a matter of life or death. I realized I could not wait for the resident. I grabbed a metal stool and smashed the emergency cabinet, took out the adrenalin, and gave her a shot subcutaneously. I prepared a syringe of intravenous hydrocortisone and gave her that as well. She was cyanotic, turning blue. I started to give her artificial respiration. At that point, the resident rushed in and gave her a second adrenaline shot, while I was administering respiration. To our great relief, she started to recover. We moved her to the emergency ward and kept her in the hospital for two days, until we were sure she was okay. The director of the Student Health Center praised me for my quick thinking and action. I never forgot this experience. An anaphylactic reaction is one of the most serious and frightening emergencies the physician can face. I would experience this emergency only twice again in my medical career.

In our fourth year, we applied for our internship. I was accepted at Reading Hospital. It had been years of hard work, sleepless nights, setbacks and delays, and living more on dreams and faith than an excess of food or money. Then the day arrived. Medical school was over.

Graduation was an extremely happy day. As I sat there with my class and heard the Hippocratic Oath read, I thanked God for seeing me through to that moment. I prayed that whatever I did as a physician would always be for the good of the patient. After graduation, I hugged and kissed Joanne, then my mother,

Aunt Alice, and finally my mother-in-law, who said that she was proud of me for the first time since I had known her.

I was extremely grateful to my wife. Joanne carried the burden of living on the thin side of poverty and caring for the children for so many years. We still had to go through internship and my pathology residency. I knew she would be with me, whatever the hardships we faced, and that she would rejoice with me in the good times. Hugging her that day, I knew this wonderful woman was one of God's finest creations and a great gift to me. Without her help and support, I would never have reached that proud day.

CHAPTER 7

Administration of a Bitter Pill

At the completion of medical school, each young MD has attained a great deal of scientific knowledge and a degree of clinical knowledge. The internship is designed to provide a controlled environment in which to convert that knowledge to an understanding of the practice of medicine. Being a physician means learning many skills. You cannot learn this from books or lectures, as medicine is both a science and an art, and you can only learn an art by practice. It is the combination of the intern's medical training, the hospital, and the staff of competent senior physicians which create practical experience. Here a young doctor will take on the awesome responsibility for the care of a fellow human for the first time. As an intern, you learn what it means to be available night and day for your patients. You face fatigue, frustration, and even fear. Often you will confront the unknown, and you will be taxed to the limit of your ability.

The hospital internship was known as a rotating internship. Every intern rotated through all of the medical specialties during the course of one year. Each intern was given a roster of the services, or specialties, that he would be on and the dates. My first service was obstetrics and gynecology. We lived in intern quarters on the third floor of the hospital which consisted of small private rooms, a general bathroom, a recreation room, and a kitchen, which was always well stocked with food. The key piece of equipment was the telephone, the bane of our existence.

The Emergency Room was the most demanding service in the hospital. We were on duty twenty-four hours a day. From patient to patient, we never knew what was going to happen next. At times, there would be an hour to relax, and then five patients would come in at once. The next moment, there would be a car accident with lacerations and fractures. The emergency crew in those days was limited to one intern and one nurse.

One Saturday night, we were busy with accidents, drunks, and the usual walk-in illnesses and bleeding gashes. We had only one student nurse, working with the ER head nurse, Fern, and myself, managing three patients in the emergency ward. I had just started to sew up a laceration on an intoxicated woman who had fallen down a flight of stairs. The fact that she had also broken her thumb did not seem to matter too much to her. She was more concerned about the cut on her mouth and whether or not it was going to leave a scar. I had just placed the first stitch when a distraught mother came in with an even more distraught young lady. The younger woman was walking awkwardly with her legs far apart. Fern guided them into a side room to see what the problem was, because they were so upset. When Fern came out, she was wide-eyed. This was very unusual for Fern, for she was a veteran Emergency Room nurse. I believed she had seen everything conceivable that could happen in this city of a hundred thousand people.

Fern was very prim and bristled at any type of sexual discussion in her presence. She came into the room as I was closing the drunken woman's laceration. I asked Fern what the problem was with the mother and daughter.

"Doctor," she said, "I think you have to see this girl as soon as possible. She will explain the problem." Within fifteen minutes, I had closed the wound, removed my gloves, and walked into the side room.

The girl, whose name was Amy, was sobbing, and the mother looked about as distressed as I've ever seen a mother, short of those who had lost a child. I sat down next to the girl. She looked at me with her red, tear-filled eyes and said, "Didn't the nurse tell you my problem?"

"No," I replied, "would you please tell me what your problem is?"

She had covered her legs with her coat. She removed the coat and pulled up her dress, and opened her legs slightly. There, protruding from her vagina, was what appeared to be a soda pop bottle. Amy said she had tried to remove the bottle, but that it was stuck on something inside of her. It hurt anytime she pulled on it. On the trip to the hospital, she said she was holding the bottle between her legs to keep it from hurting her. I wasn't quite sure how the bottle was stuck in her, or on to which part of her anatomy. It had fastened itself within the vaginal canal, so there could be only two options: either it fastened onto the vaginal wall, or the cervix of the uterus. I told Fern to move her to one of the operating tables for a more comprehensive examination and to call the gynecologist on service. We were going to need his help. Once the girl was on the table, positioned to be examined, I discovered that there was a minimum of blood present. The bottle occupied the entire vaginal orifice. I could not use the standard vaginal speculum to examine her. I waited for the gynecologist on duty to discuss the case with him. To my great delight, Dr. Brubaker, one of the best gynecologists in the hospital and a terrific person, was on duty. He had a cool head and was a most competent gynecologist-obstetrician. He was known to the professionals as Bru.

Bru's presence in the room inspired everyone with confidence. He had a calming quality. Before he began to examine the girl, we heard the rest of the story. Amy had had unprotected intercourse with her boyfriend about two hours before she came to the hospital. Since they had not used contraception, the boyfriend suggested that she douche with 7-Up to prevent getting pregnant. She was only eighteen, an unsophisticated college freshman, without prior sexual experience. Her boyfriend had advised her to shake up the 7-Up bottle and place it about halfway into her vagina, then remove it, shake it up again, and put it in as far as it would go. She was unable to remove the bottle after this last insertion.

Both Bru and I understood immediately. The exhausted liquid–foam had created a vacuum, pulling the vaginal tissue and/or the cervix into the opening of the bottle. Bru dismantled a speculum, separating the top and the bottom. He was able to expand the vagina enough to see that the bottle was tightly impinged on the bottom lip of the cervix. He made a thorough examination of her chest with a stethoscope. I wondered exactly why he did this. He suggested that we step out to discuss our options.

Bru sat down, lit a cigarette, poured himself a cup coffee, and said, "This is really one for the books. I really don't know how we are going to get this off. Somehow we need to break that vacuum."

He told me about an article he had read in a medical journal shortly after World War II, about an unusual cause of death following sexual activity. In England, several deaths resulted from air embolisms formed when soldiers, in a sexual frenzy, blew air into a partner's vaginal canal. There were three documented deaths before the article was written.

Bru explained, "I was concerned that using effervescent liquid in the vaginal canal could potentially lead to an air embolism."

"Is this why you examined her chest?" I asked.

"Yes," he replied, "though clinically, she didn't have any sign of respiratory distress."

At first he suggested using a tube, such as a catheter, to try to snake between the rim of the bottle and the cervix. We realized this was impractical. I thought about drilling a hole in the bottom of the bottle and mentioned it.

"How would you do this?" Bru asked.

"We simply take a diamond-tip drill and drill a hole into the bottom of the bottle."

"Where are we going to get a diamond-tip drill, particularly at this time of night? I'm sure the hospital does not have one," Bru replied.

"Yes," I agreed, "that is not an item most maintenance shops would have on hand, let alone an OR." I remembered that when I worked in the bacteriology laboratory of this hospital, we used to write on glass slides with a diamond-tip pencil. The pencil was always in the left-hand upper drawer of the microbiologist's desk. The microbiologist was affectionately known as "Bugs." I remembered that he was methodical and orderly. Most likely that pencil was still in the same place. I mentioned this to Bru and then ran up to the microbiologist's laboratory to find the diamond-tip pencil. It was exactly where I thought it was. I grabbed it and hastened back to Emergency.

"Here it is. This will do the trick," I said. "Now, all we need is a quarter-inch electric drill, which I'm sure the maintenance shop has." The maintenance shop was down in the tunnels that ran underneath the hospital, at least two blocks away from Emergency. I left Bru with our patient and ran the distance to get a drill. I woke up the maintenance man and explained that I needed a drill for an emergency and that he would not be the person to operate it. I explained that the medical procedure required that I had to use the drill. He was giving me a hard time, so I told him exactly why I needed the drill. He understood, gave me the drill, and said he wanted to come to watch. Already in motion, I told him that this would be impossible and ran the two blocks underground back to Emergency.

Bru had wrapped the bottle in saline-soaked 4x4 gauze and wrapped surgical tape around the bottom of the bottle in case it cracked or shattered. Bru held the bottle as I applied pressure with the diamond tip pencil and drill. I was drilling a cone-shaped hole. It was slow going. I had to move the drill in a circular motion in order to widen the hole, since only a small portion of the tip of the pencil was a diamond. We added a few drops of saline to keep the dust down and to help control the temperature of the glass. After about six or seven minutes, we were making good progress, but we still had a way to go. The girl was feeling no pain. She had stopped crying and asked if her mother was still in the waiting room. Fern confirmed that her mother was still waiting.

After almost ten more minutes, Bru announced, "It's off!" We had drilled through the base of the bottle. It gave up its trapped cervix with no trouble and had not cracked. Clear of the bottle, Bru was able to examine the cervix and determine what sort of damage she had suffered. There was a large blister on the end of her cervix associated with a certain amount of hemorrhage at the base, and a few drops of blood were seen in the vaginal canal. All in all, she had suffered surprisingly little damage. Bru decided to keep her overnight and to reexamine her in the morning. As he was writing the admission orders, I went to reassure her mother that everything was okay.

The mother, a matronly, quiet woman, was much relieved that her daughter was not going to have any serious long-term problem as a result of what had happened. She could not believe that her daughter, always a serious student, was "doing these things." She was terribly embarrassed by the incident and hoped it would not get into the newspaper. There was always a reporter lurking around Emergency on Saturday evenings. She felt terribly let down by her daughter but was concerned about her health and well-being. I explained that risky behavior might be expected as children experience the new freedoms of college life. We, as parents, hope it won't, believing that trouble only happens to somebody else. I told her not to feel bad about her daughter, who would need her mother's moral support.

After the mother left, Amy was transferred to her room to rest for the night. We all went back to the business of taking care of the accidents, the drunks, and the acutely ill. Sometime around four o'clock, things eased off, and I was able to get a few hours of sleep.

Having breakfast at the cafeteria, I found the talk of the incident had spread to most of the hospital personnel, particularly the student nurses who were all abuzz. I was sure that Bru would discharge our patient early, and I felt I needed to see the young lady before she left. When I came into her room, Amy greeted me meekly, with some embarrassment. I sat on the chair near her bed and asked her how she felt, if she had any pain or discomfort. She said she felt fine and was ready to go home.

I looked at her for moment and said, "Dr. Brubaker will be in shortly to discharge you after he examines you. I'm sure you're going to be okay. Amy, I would like to tell you one or two little things about boys, and how you might be able to avoid something like this in the future. Do you mind if I speak with you?"

"No," she said, "I would appreciate anything . . . if you could tell me . . . I am so dumb about these things . . . I never had a boyfriend in high school, because I had to study real hard and work after school. It's not that I was not interested in boys . . . I just didn't have time."

I nodded that I understood. Amy was about five foot five, brunette, and wore glasses. She was an attractive young woman. Since she was so shy, I chose my words carefully.

"You are not dumb, Amy, you are just an inexperienced young lady. The first thing you should know is that most boys are more sexually oriented than girls, for a lot of different reasons, which I won't go into right now. As a rule, girls are looking for more stable relationships than boys, since girls are primarily oriented to love, marriage, and family. Things can get a little mixed up when a boy and girl meet, and they are not sure of the relationship that they have, or are going to have.

"This is what I have learned about good men. When a man is interested in a woman seriously, the very first thing he will do is to try to protect her in every possible situation. This means preventing other men from dating her or trying to harm her in any way. The second thing that he will do is to bring you small gifts, usually food. This is actually bred into him for hundreds of thousands, if not millions, of years. This is nature's way of telling you that this man is interested in your welfare. Sometimes he may bring you a little trinket, but nothing expensive, nothing that will overwhelm you or attempt to make a big impression. A man who is genuinely interested in you for a long-term relationship, and by that I mean marriage, will not press you for sexual favors. Instinctively, he knows that sexual activity can be potentially harmful to you, and he will not want to risk harming you. He wants to protect you and keep you healthy to be his future wife. Now, I realize these are very simple things, but I have seen this with many, many men. I can assure you that if you follow these signs, you will be more likely to find a good life partner than not."

Amy sat there and listened intently to what I said and seemed to relax. I was talking to her as one human being to another without judgment.

"When you are discharged from the hospital and are back in school, if you have any problem that I could help you with, Amy, please call me at the hospital. I am sure that Dr. Brubaker wants to see you one more time at his office. He is an exceptionally fine doctor, and I would recommend that you do whatever he tells you."

She looked at me, took a breath, and said, "I really didn't want to do that, Doctor. But he kept pestering me and telling me that everybody was doing it and I was foolish not to. He said there were plenty of girls on the campus who would do it if I would not."

I told her that was one of the oldest lines that boys used. If a boy ever said that to her again, she would know immediately that he was not the kind of boy who would make a lifelong companion. That sort of boy is only interested in using her for sex, for his own conquest, and would likely drop her and move on, using the same line with other girls. She thanked me for taking the time to talk to her. When Bru came into the room, she was happy to see him. I smiled and said, "Good-bye, Amy. I wish you good luck."

I did not see Amy again for almost fifteen years, when I ran into her at the department store during the Christmas season. She recognized me and came up to introduce herself. I remembered her because of the unusual case. She was a social worker now, had married an attorney, and had two children. She was very happy. Amy told me that she had often thought about what I had said to her over the years.

"Doctor, what you said to me in the hospital really helped me, several times. I remembered what you told me, and because of it, I believe I avoided a few dangerous situations with boys."

"I am so happy to hear that, Amy," I said, "and thank you for letting me know how well your life turned out."

Driving home, I thought of all the possibilities that this young lady had faced while in college, and all of those stupid, selfish boys who are in college for no other reason than to have a good time, raise hell, and seduce inexperienced young girls. Although Amy had not escaped totally unscathed, she had weathered the storm of her inexperience and was able to plot a course safely through the rocks and shoals of life until she met her lifelong partner. I thought of how many girls have jeopardized their whole lives for the attention of one teenage boy, and how slim the margin is between happiness and disaster.

After Emergency Room service, I moved to pediatrics. Pediatrics was one of the more interesting services in the hospital. Most of the illnesses are acute, though at times you see chronic illnesses and fatal diseases. I learned a great deal from the pediatricians at Reading Hospital. Dr. Herman Kotzen showed me how to do circumcisions in a much easier way than the way I was taught in medical school. Once I started to do these, I was able to supplement my intern salary by doing circumcisions for several of the doctors. For this service, I was paid ten dollars per procedure. One week, I made one hundred dollars, which was like finding a gold mine.

Most of the interns had a little difficulty with the hospital pharmacist whenever they ordered a high-priced drug for a charity patient. In most cases, he would request that the staff physician approve this order before he would fill it. I think he did not have a good feeling about interns, because interns seemed to be oblivious to the cost of medications. Knowing he held us in relatively low esteem, most of us considered the pharmacist to be unfriendly.

While I was making rounds in the pediatric ward one evening, a two-year-old boy was admitted with laryngotracheobronchitis, commonly called croup. He was the pharmacist's son. The boy was acutely ill, but under the care of a very good pediatrician, who told me to keep a keen eye on this little boy and to check on him at least every half hour. This did not prove to be easy. I had to get up every half hour to come down to the ward to check on this patient. I went to night supper at 10:30 and checked on him again a little after 11. His temperature was still elevated. His breathing was labored, but his color was good. I was sitting with him when I received a call from Emergency. They were admitting a five-year-old boy with abdominal pain. I got a history from his mother, did the physical examination, and ordered the laboratory tests. The signs indicated mesenteric adenitis. Mesenteric adenitis is believed to be a viral condition that causes an inflammation of the lymph nodes surrounding the bowel. The signs and symptoms of mesenteric adenitis mimic the signs and symptoms of appendicitis. It is one of the differential diagnoses you must consider whenever you have a young patient with abdominal pain, but I waited until the laboratory tests returned before I felt certain about my diagnosis.

It was 1:30 in the morning before I went back to check on the pharmacist's son. His condition had worsened. His breathing was labored, and his color was ashen grey. He was in acute respiratory distress. I picked him up and told the nurse to call Dr. Phil Wiest. I also ordered the nurse to get an anesthetist to the OR right away.

Taking the child in my arms, I ran with the boy to the elevator and carried him to the OR. An anesthetist was waiting.

We put him on the table with his shoulders on a pillow. His head was held back so that the trachea was forced into a prominent position. The nurse tried to aspirate him to help his breathing, but her efforts were to no avail. While we were working on him, Dr. Wiest entered the room and immediately started the tracheotomy. A tracheotomy on a two-year-old is a very precise procedure, because the trachea is so small. Dr. Wiest was skilled in otorhinolaryngology, a specialty now known as ENT, for ear, nose, and throat. He was able to perform the delicate insertion successfully to aspirate the boy. In a few minutes, the child's breathing had improved as did his color. We all breathed a sigh of relief and thanked God that this little life was saved. I sat with Dr. Wiest for a half hour after we finished the surgery. He stayed to make sure the boy was out of danger, and then we moved him to the intensive care unit.

The nurses had called his parents who arrived at the hospital shortly after we had completed the surgery. Their son was much improved, but was not yet out of the woods. Dr. Wiest and I sat with the pharmacist and his wife, explaining that the tracheotomy was lifesaving. They were very grateful. Dr. Wiest told them that if I had not been watching over their child, most likely he would not have survived. The pharmacist looked at me with tears in his eyes, shook my hand, and thanked me profusely. I believe his impression of interns changed considerably that evening.

Just as the holiday season was beginning, a six-year-old boy named Al came into the pediatric ward. Al was a delightful, pleasant little boy who was full of life and excited about school. He had a horrifying diagnosis of a medulloblastoma, a type of brain tumor located in the cerebellum, the part of the brain that controls balance and other complex motor functions. Medulloblastoma is the most common cancerous central nervous system tumor in children. It occurs most commonly between ages three and eight, but can be seen at any age. Al had a history of repeated episodes of vomiting and a morning headache. As the disease progressed, he developed a stumbling gait with frequent falls. We estimated that the tumor had been there at least four or five months before the diagnosis was made.

Al was one of the most outgoing patients in the pediatric ward. He giggled and clapped whenever I performed one of my new string tricks or showed him how I could make a tall tree out of a rolled up newspaper. He was very upbeat about our ability to cure his problem. After he was in the hospital for a few days, I came in to check him prior to surgery. "Hello there, Al!" I greeted him as I approached his bed. He looked at me with a love that I'll never forget and said with a radiant smile, "Today you're going to make me better, aren't you, Doctor?"

I knew his chances were extremely slim, but he was in the hands of Herb Johnson, one of the best neurosurgeons I had ever met. I looked at him and patted him on the shoulder and said, "Al, you bet we are going to do everything we can to help you." He smiled and waved good-bye as he was wheeled down the hall to the elevator heading to the OR.

I waited to hear Dr. Johnson's report of his findings. When I saw him come out of the OR, I knew it had not gone well. Herb Johnson also loved children. I could see that he was shaken. With as much calm as he could muster, he said, "He died on the table."

I did not want to hear that. I was very attached to this little boy, and I felt we had failed him as medical professionals. Even though I knew the odds were stacked against him and only a miracle could have saved him, I had never felt worse in my life as a physician. I went to my room and cried. As I prayed for his little soul, I knew that Al was with God. When I thought about the terrible pain that his parents were going through, I prayed that they would be comforted, in some way. I did not understand death, or my role as a physician in helping those who were dying and those who were losing loved ones. I learned from losing little Al that it is not the patients who have pain with a death, but the survivors.

The holiday season was approaching. The hospital staff could choose to have off either Christmas or New Year's Day. The young, single interns chose New Year's, so we old, married guys could have Christmas Day with our families.

New Year's broke on us like a hurricane. We were covering two or more services each. The rest of the interns were off, so we had to do double and triple duty. I was on backup for the emergency service which seemed to rage both day and night during the holidays. New Year's Eve was an absolute nightmare. We had so many auto accidents, falling drunks in bars and fights with lacerations. I dimly remember it was well after four o'clock in the morning before things slowed down. We were still on our feet at breakfast time. One of the interns who had been assisting in surgery all through the night fell sound asleep in his breakfast plate, and we had a hell of a time waking him up.

It was February, the last month of the ancient Roman calendar. I remembered that *februa* was the Latin word for purification. As I was tossing this in my mind, it occurred to me that I had not checked on my residency with the pathology department since my internship started, and time was moving quickly. I decided to go up to the department to discuss my upcoming residency with the head of pathology, Dr. Richard Sycamore.

My decision to intern where I was had been because the hospital had reciprocity with Dr. Philip Custer, the leading pathologist/hematologist in the United States. I would get to spend one year working at Presbyterian Hospital with Dr. Custer, whom I had the pleasure of meeting in my third year of medical school.

I looked forward to a discussion with Dr. Sycamore about my upcoming residency in pathology. I wanted to make sure there was nothing I had forgotten to do and that I would know what the starting date would be. I was totally unprepared for what followed. I was quite used to obstacles, bumps in the road, rocks and hard places, disappointments of all types, and unexpected outcomes from those things that I thought were cut and dried. In my wildest imagination, I could not have predicted what was to follow when I walked into that office. It would change my entire life's plan. I was about to learn a very costly lesson in life, one that would forever color how I would relate to people.

As I entered Dr. Sycamore' office, he was sitting at the microscope table with Dr. Ted Root, his assistant and a pathology resident.

"Hi, Richard," I greeted, "I thought I would stop by for a cup of coffee and discuss my residency."

He looked up from his microscope. His expression was one I had never seen on him. His face was fixed, not so much a look of anger, but oddly, one of disapproval. Richard was normally a friendly person, though somewhat reserved, so I was taken aback by his expression. I wasn't prepared at all for his reply.

"What residency?" he asked, his voice flat.

The impact of that response left me speechless for a moment. I was used to being treated very much like a colleague when I went into the pathology department. The atmosphere was suddenly hostile, and my presence was clearly the reason.

"Richard," I said, keeping my voice even, "you must remember that I came to visit you in my last year of medical school, before I applied for an internship, to discuss the possibility of a residency in pathology with you."

He acknowledged that with a slight nod of his head and, lowering his voice, answered, "Yes, but you never filled out an application."

I tried to respond with some semblance of normalcy. "You told me at the time that there was no need for me to fill out an application, that you had all the background on me that you needed. You told me that I should go ahead and apply for the internship here because the residency in pathology would be assured."

He now stood up, moving away from the microscope table. Dr. Sycamore walked over to me and said, "There is no residency for you, Peter. All the places have been filled for next year. You will have to apply through the usual channels."

This cold, definitive reply froze me on the spot. I looked at him in disbelief and replied, "Richard, we both know it is too late for me to apply for residency any place else. I came to this hospital as an intern only because of the residency program, and to have an opportunity to work with Dr. Custer. I know we discussed this and you had agreed."

Moving back to his seat, he replied, perfunctorily, "There's nothing I can do about it. There are no residencies available."

In that instant, my life changed. I turned and left the room without saying another word. Walking down the hall in a daze, I realized that the decision had been made from a higher level. The only reason that could have affected this decision was an incident that occurred early in my internship.

I'd had a run-in with a nurse who was disdainful of interns. She had ordered intravenous fluids, saline and glucose, over my name on the chart for a patient with congestive heart failure and diabetes, without checking with me. The patient almost died. I had refused to sign the order. The head nurse refused to admit any wrongdoing, and the medical staff did not support me. Standing on principle was not appreciated by the hospital hierarchy. I did not realize at the time that this incident would have a profound effect on the rest of my life. Beginning immediately.

I went to the medical library reading room where I could be alone for a while. What was I to do? My whole professional life was research, specifically research in hematological diseases. Now, in an instant, this was gone. What was I going to tell Joanne when I went home that evening? How could we plan for the future?

I sat there and prayed for guidance, but my thoughts were beset with questions of why. I knew that God had not abandoned me, but for some reason, he was pushing me into another pathway.

I had always believed in the truth and in doing the right thing. Now, I discovered that that very principle had destroyed my plans for the future. It had made me a pariah in the hospital. Essentially, I was an untouchable. I could see now why only a few of the staff members had been friendly to me of late. The word had come down from the top that I was no longer welcome at this hospital. The more I thought of it, the angrier I became, and I decided I would fight it. This would prove to be a very bad decision.

The winter passed, and when spring approached, we had to make application to take our state medical license examination. This application required a certificate from the hospital of satisfactory completion of your internship. It seemed that everybody had theirs but me. When I inquired as to where mine was, the medical director informed me that they "were working on it." I smelled a rat. Later that afternoon, I got a page over the hospital system to come to the medical library. I wondered what that was all about, but I went immediately to the library, and there was my staunchest supporter and physician friend, Dr. Merle B. DeWire.

I greeted him cordially, happy to see a friend. But his face was a mask of grave concern. He asked me to sit down at the table in a manner that told me this meeting was one of great seriousness. Even still, his eyes were sad with the empathy of a pediatrician about to give a child a shot, and he addressed me by the childhood nickname he'd given me.

"Jerry, you are in deep doo-doo!" my friend said. "The hospital is not going to give you a certificate of completion, and in fact, they are going to give you a letter of incompetency."

"What?!" Beyond shocked, I was first horrified and then driven to extreme anger, like a wild animal trapped in a corner. "That nurse . . ." I hissed, "almost killed my patient with IVs I never ordered! She admitted that she ordered them, and I couldn't even report her to anybody. The entire administration refused to make any move to discipline her. I will sue this hospital!" I exclaimed.

Dr. DeWire rose from his seat. He got me by the arm and literally raised me from the chair. In a very firm voice, he said, "You will do nothing of the kind. You have no idea how high, deep, and wide the ties run from this hospital into the community. You have no money for lawyers, and these people will slaughter you. What you're going to do is to get your butt up to that record room and sign that #$@! chart, or I'm going to kick your ass all the way up there. I am not going to allow you to throw away all your years of study for some impossible-to-attain principle."

I said nothing. Dr. DeWire was the only true friend I had on that staff. He was a genuine, strong man, one who also believed in principles, and one who would never desert a friend. He had no obligation to me, yet he had been our family doctor for many years, before leaving general practice to specialize in urology. He stayed in touch with me while I was in medical school, always encouraging me. Now, in the face of this baffling and unconscionable injustice, his bold intervention literally saved my medical career.

I went with him to the record room, requested the chart, and signed it. We left the record room, and Dr. DeWire said, "Now, you're all right. Everything will be okay. I'll see you later."

He left to go to his office. As I was walking down the hall, I got another page, to report to the medical director's office. When I walked into Dr. Locust's office, he stood up, came over to me, put his arm around me, and said, "Son, you did the right thing."

I had no words to reply. I turned on my heel and left his office. As I walked down the hall without a destination, I felt anger, despair, hopelessness, and fear. Finally, I sank into a chair in an empty room, with questions spinning in my head. Where would I go? What would I do?

I don't recall how long I sat there, thinking and feeling very much alone and betrayed. Then I thought of Joanne, at home with little Steven and Patti, and in that moment, I realized again that I was blessed. Sure, this was a problem. I would most likely not be a pathologist, but I could still practice medicine as a general practitioner, until I found my true calling.

I stood up and headed for the elevator. I walked into the small, nondenominational chapel on the second floor, secure on my feet yet I knelt. In the quiet atmosphere, I prayed a prayer of thanksgiving. Peace began to settle on me, and with absolute clarity, I understood the one real truth that had come out of this experience. I had gotten this far only with God's help, and whatever the Lord had planned for me, I was ready to obey.

My intern days were over. I took our three-day state board examination in June. I would have to wait until August or September to learn whether I passed or not.

During that summer, I worked at another hospital, in the pediatric department and the emergency room. I added some diagnostic skills working with Dr. Kagan, the son of the jeweler from whom I had purchased my wife's engagement ring many years before. In early August, I received word that I had passed the state board, as did all of the interns. I was able to practice medicine and surgery, as Peter T. Pugliese, MD.

When my license arrived at the end of September, Joanne and I sat at our kitchen table looking at it. This is what we had worked for since the day we were married. This little piece of parchment was the key to our future life. All the years of struggling, studying, deprivation, and hopeful expectation seemed to be embodied in that little piece of paper. This is what we had talked about, thought about, and worked for. Now there it was on our kitchen table, just a little piece of parchment. We had completed one long journey. We were moving right into another, only this one would last until the end of our lives. Whether we felt relief or excitement I do not remember, but I do know that we were tremendously happy.

These transcendental moments of pure happiness are best savored when shared with the person you love most in the world. There exists a moment when time seems to stand still, a moment of sheer bliss, a moment that you know you will never experience again. It is a moment made of a conjunction of many elements, all coming together at the same time. We held each other, treasuring that moment, and thanked God for all the wonderful blessings he had given us.

CHAPTER 8

Roots and Wings

In January of my last year of internship, when I had learned my residency would be at Reading Hospital, I went to the area to look for a home.

I was always interested in owning a farm, because it brought back such pleasant memories of the days I spent with my Uncle Howard and Aunt Lorena. On a whim, I contacted a farm agent and drove around with him looking at properties. I told him my situation. I would not be able to buy a farm in excess of $10,000. I had no idea how I would come up with even that amount. After looking at a number of places, we drove back to Reading through Bernville. He said he would like to show me a farm, though it was beyond my price. We drove over to have a look. It was a 210-acre farm with a stone manor house and a brick tenant house. Two farms had been merged by the prior owner.

Our farm, one of the oldest farms in Jefferson Township, is located approximately a mile from Bernville's center. The Kline family cemetery on the property was established in 1750. The property consisted of two adjacent farms, the Trautman farm and the Bright farm. Both families were original settlers of the Tulpehocken area. The stone foundation of an original building constructed around 1750 was still visible on the Bright farm. The stone home, built in 1829 and completed in 1831, in which we would live, was a typical Pennsylvania manor house. The home was built by John Meise who named it after his wife, "Chatrina." Even though the place had been vacant for eighteen months and needed a lot of attention, I fell in love with the old house the very first time I saw it.

The house originally had twelve rooms. The four rooms on the first floor consisted of a large kitchen, a dining room, a living room, and a sitting room. The second floor had four bedrooms, and there were two large rooms on the third floor. Sometime in the forties, three bathrooms and a powder room were added along with electricity and central heating. Four of the rooms had built-in corner cupboards, and there were originally four fireplaces. It was a very comfortable home. The lane was a dirt road half a mile long that opened onto Route 183, the main road from Bernville to Reading. When there were more than three inches of snow, the lane was completely impassable because of the wind sweeping across the fields.

Typical of Pennsylvania farms, the topography was mostly rolling hills. There were fifteen acres of relatively flat field in front of the house. A small forest separated what we call the Bottom Main from the Upper Sixty acres. The forest contained oak, poplar, sweet gum, hickory, locust, and beech. The very large, beautifully formed walnut trees were perfect for my woodworking hobby. Running quietly along the woodland was a stream known as the Little Northkill Creek, a tributary of the Northkill Creek that figured so importantly in the livelihood of the Leni-Lenape Indians. The minute I laid eyes on it, I knew this was the farm for Joanne and me. The $35,000 price was daunting, but the agent thought he could get it for $30,000. I would still need a $5,000 down payment. I thought I could borrow it from my father and pay only the interest during my internship.

That was a dream built on air. Furious with me, my father said only an idiot would think about buying a farm when he did not have a dime in the bank and no source of income for the next six months.

Dejected, I drove over to Aunt Alice's home for a cup of coffee and with luck a sandwich. I did not have enough money to buy both lunch and gas to return to Philly. It was one or the other. She was happy to see me, but she observed that I looked depressed and out of sorts. I explained the episode with my dad and my interest in the farm. She said, "Tell me about the farm."

After I described it to her, she expressed interest in seeing it. We drove to Bernville to have a look. When she saw the stone house, the gardens and all the land, she said to my great surprise, "I will let you borrow the down payment."

Again, a miracle of kindness helped me to realize my dreams.

Leaping out of my chair, I gave Aunt Alice a hug and kiss, and we drove back to Reading. I called the real estate agent and told him that I would be ready to make settlement at the end of the following week. He said he needed a $1,000 payment to secure the deal. I told him I would write a check, but he should hold it until settlement. He agreed to do so. I could not wait to tell Joanne.

During my internship, Joanne and the children lived at the farm. We had every other weekend and every third night off. On my weekends off, we hiked and explored the many acres of the farm, high into the woods and fields and down to the stream.

A quarter mile of the Northkill Creek flowed through our property. The creek was stocked yearly with trout. Many local fishermen gathered on the banks during deficiencies. Schoolboys would come every year to ask my permission to hunt muskrats along the creek. Of course, many deer made their home on our property. We enjoyed sitting on the porch and watching the abundant wildlife stirring about, looking for food, chasing a mate, or just playing and enjoying life.

In the spring, we enjoyed beautiful fields full of daisies and other wildflowers. The fields surrounding the house stretching toward the thirty acres of woodland comprised many acres of rich land for growing crops. This acreage was rented to a tenant farmer who lived in a second house on the property.

It was great to enjoy the peace on our farm. We had arrived with two small children, hoping that we would be blessed with more. My siblings and their growing families came on weekends to visit and to hunt and swim, and we always ate Sunday spaghetti dinner together with my parents, whom we'd moved into the brick house, one quarter mile (or one toddler's morning walk) down the lane.

Now I was ready to begin practicing medicine in Bernville, fully aware that the early days of practice can be difficult.

New doctors often spend day after day dreaming of future success, only to go home in the evening without an extra dime in their pockets. A line is cast and a new doctor hopes to get a nibble soon. We storm heaven with prayers that the meager amount of survival money borrowed from our parents will last until the practice grows.

"Doctor!" A woman's voice rang out in the waiting room and echoed down the hall. "Help me. My son has just been hurt."

It was my first patient. I leaped up and hastened to the waiting room. There I found a very distressed young lady holding the door open and pointing outside to her auto. There in the backseat lay an eight-year-old boy with flaming red hair, who was crying loudly and holding his left arm. I examined the boy in the car. He had a fractured clavicle. Gently lifting him to his feet, I walked him into the office and had him sit on the treatment table. The mother, wide-eyed and anxious, was wringing her hands and hyperventilating. The first order of business was to have her sit down so she didn't faint. Carefully removing the boy's baseball shirt, I saw a classic left mid-clavicle fracture. Once I was able to get him to stop crying, I brought the shoulders back into position and applied a figure-eight ace bandage. I gave him a couple of aspirin tablets. He sat quietly while I obtained a history and patient information from his mother. Her son had been standing on the sideline at the baseball diamond. Another boy was warming up, swinging his bat back and forth. He connected with the red-haired boy's shoulder. It was purely an accident.

I had no idea what to charge for this service or how the patient would pay. His mother had Blue Cross and Blue Shield. In those days, a fractured clavicle was billed out at thirty-five dollars. Since my office fee at that time was three dollars, this visit was an incredible windfall, even though I would not see a check for at least three weeks. I told the mother to call me if her son had any problem and that I would like to see him in a week. To my dismay, I did not have any forms to submit to Blue Shield. I assumed Dr. Bertolette had a good supply in his office which I could get from him the next day. I went home that evening with a smile on my face and related the whole episode in great detail to Joanne. We knew we were going to make it. It was a good day.

I whiled away the next two days with a drug salesman and a car salesman. Not very propitious. The next morning at 7:00, I got a call from a soft-spoken, deeply concerned woman whose son was having what she described as a grand mal seizure. Unable to bring him to the office, she asked if I would make a housecall, about eight miles away. This family lived on Route 419 about a mile or two south of Rehrersburg. She described the house, so it was easy to find. After obtaining directions, I jumped into my car and zoomed out the lane. As I drove, I reviewed everything

I knew about treating epilepsy and controlling seizures. Old school doctors advised lighting up a cigar and taking a leisurely walk around the block before seeing a patient having an epileptic attack. By the time you reached the patient, the seizure would have passed. In the late fifties, there was no known treatment for controlling epileptic seizures.

When I arrived, the mother, Marie, was at the door with her child, who was still having a seizure. He was a little boy about three or four years old who looked ill and exhausted. I placed him on the sofa and took a vial of Secobarbital™ from my medical bag, which I administered to the boy intravenously. Within less than a minute, his seizures stopped, and he was breathing more easily. Only then could I talk with the mother to obtain some history. The little boy's name was Tommy. He had been well until he was about eighteen months old, when he came down with a high fever caused by an upper respiratory infection. He had a convulsion. His parents rushed him to the doctor's office for treatment. Whenever Tommy had an infection with a fever during the following two years, he had experienced convulsions.

I was impressed by the mother's concern and love for her child. Marie spoke with tenderness and devotion to her little boy. A very gentle lady, she had a quiet elegance, though she was a very plain woman. Her straight, dark black hair was held back by hairpins above her ears. Her tentative smile gave me the impression that she hoped everything would be all right, but she wasn't quite sure. The intensity of her anxiety was palpable. As we spoke, her husband rushed into the room. He had come home from work to be with her. Marie's husband, Lee, was a handsome young man. His face was creased with concern. I could see they were deeply in love. He comforted his wife, who seemed to blame herself for Tommy's problems.

I sat with them gathering as much history as I could while Tommy slept peacefully on the sofa. His family physician had placed him on an antibiotic. When I examined him, I saw that he had pharyngitis and otitis media, which is a sore throat and middle ear infection. I could add nothing to his treatment except to try to find the cause of the epilepsy. I planned to contact their doctor to tell him what I had done. I suggested they see a pediatrician for a general workup for Tommy. I recommended Dr. Harvey Leinbach and indicated I would discuss that with their physician as well.

I had not seen a case of epilepsy in medical school. Though it is not a rare condition, only one case to my knowledge was treated in the hospital during my internship. *Status epilepticus* is a convulsion that lasts at least five minutes but can last as long as thirty minutes. This little boy had suffered a serious upper respiratory infection with high fever that damaged his brain. Each convulsive seizure deprives the brain of oxygen and that destroys neurons. His future did not look good. This caring couple had won me over, but I assumed I would not see them again. They would continue with Dr. Leinbach and Marie's current physician. As often as I could, I referred patients to the specialists in Reading, many of whom went on to devise historic techniques, treatments, or instruments.

By the fourth or fifth month, my practice had grown. I was seeing patients every day, but the office was by no means filled to capacity at any time. Joanne was pleased by the way our income was slowly building. We could meet our bills and begin to put a little money aside to pay my medical school debts. It was a hand-to-mouth affair at the very best.

Around ten o'clock one evening, I received a call from a woman who identified herself as Mrs. Leroy Kline. The Kline family was one of the oldest families in Bernville. They had perpetual rights to visit the cemetery on our farm whenever they desired. Her husband, Leroy Kline, a slight, dapper salesman for a school book publishing company, was the current patriarch of the family.

Mrs. Kline was very agitated and concerned that her husband might be having a heart attack. She asked if I could come to see him immediately at their farm near Bernville.

When I arrived at their house, the front door was open as arranged. Mrs. Kline was standing at the top of the stairs wringing her hands. Her husband was sitting in a chair in respiratory distress. He was perspiring profusely, and his face was a mask of pain and fear. I questioned him about his symptoms, then examined him, and found that he was in the early stages of congestive heart failure. He had not had a heart attack, but he had to go to the hospital, because his heart exhibited strain and needed treatment. I did not use the ominous term "heart failure" with the Klines. When Mr. Kline began to talk to me, I suggested that he conserve his energy and promised further discussions in the morning. The ambulance arrived, and we packed him off to the hospital.

In those days, we did not have cardiologists. The internists did double duty as cardiologists and medical specialists. I told Dr. Philip Rettew, a consultant on the case, that I would work up the patient that evening and would call him later if I needed his assistance.

My patient was feeling much better in the morning after treatment with digitalis and diuretics. I suggested that he stay home for at least two to three weeks to rest up and regain his strength. Dr. Rettew felt he would not need to see Mr. Kline again. I spent quite a bit of time with Mr. Kline during the next five days, much of which we spent discussing the history of Bernville, the Kline family, and Catholicism. As I have said, there is a very strong aversion to Catholicism in Berks County among the Pennsylvania Dutch. Leroy felt the aversion to Catholicism was the result of Catholic persecution of Protestants during the Reformation in Europe. I agreed with him. My agreement was a turning point in our relationship. His attitude toward me changed considerably for the positive.

An influx of new patients, directly or indirectly related to the Kline family, continued in the following weeks and months. I saw Leroy several times in the office as he continued to improve and finally returned to work. I was feeling confident that our practice would grow and that I would earn a place in the Bernville community.

Though money was by no means pouring in, I needed to add an autoclave, an apparatus for sterilizing instruments, to the office equipment. Dr. Bertolette sterilized his needles with alcohol soaks, standard practice in many medical offices in Berks County. I had learned in medical school that alcohol does not kill bacterial spores, which can only be killed with high temperature dry heat or high temperature moist heat and pressure. Even a small autoclave is an expensive piece of equipment. I purchased one and explained to Dr. Bertolette that he was welcome to use it. He seemed to resent the fact that I did not discuss the autoclave with him before I purchased it, even though he was not contributing to the expenses. In a few days, he seemed to settle down, but things were not what they seemed.

"What the hell?!" Opening the door to my waiting room on a Saturday morning, I found an empty room. Nothing but a bunch of dust fuzzies greeted me as I stepped into the room, not a single stick of furniture. I hastened back to the treatment area and found the same state of affairs—empty, deserted, and a barren office except for my desk, my chair, and a few books. When I had office hours Thursday morning and afternoon, the office was furnished. Sometime on Friday, Dr. Bertolette had left, kit and caboodle. When three patients arrived, I had to leave them standing in the waiting room. Frantically, I called our local furniture store, which was also the funeral home, and spoke to Mr. Robert Kirkhoff. In twenty minutes, he arrived with fifteen folding chairs and a small sofa. Later on that morning, Bob added a coffee table and a few magazines. I still had no examining tables or any surgical equipment. My desktop served as an examining table, allowing me to see a few patients.

Between patients, I called our local medical equipment supplier and explained my predicament. He told me to come down, and they would be able to outfit me that afternoon. Not having a cash reserve, I could not buy the equipment. The supplier assured me that would not be a problem. I could pay for the office furnishings over time. I muddled through the morning. At noon, Joanne and I drove into Reading to look at some new equipment. We were like kids in a candy shop. I chose a hydraulic surgical table, a medical examining table, and a gynecological examining table, a pediatric examining table with a built-in scale, blood pressure apparatus, and a number of the surgical instruments, suture material, bandages, and so forth. Altogether, the bill was more than seven thousand dollars. We gasped when we saw the total, but the owner assured us we would have time to make the payments. To my amazement, he left it to my ability to pay without giving me a payment schedule. By Monday morning, we were resplendent in our newly furnished office. A rug, a few pictures in the waiting room along with two comfortable chairs and a larger sofa, and we were ready for the patients.

I hired my first employee around this time. Prior to hiring her, I sometimes had the assistance of my wife and my Aunt Alice. Aunt Alice was a strange mixture of kindness, frugality, and multiple prejudices. Not having gone beyond the eighth grade handicapped her in many ways. During the war, she became used to making good money. She decided to become a practical nurse. Not able to leave the care of her mother, she took correspondence courses. Eventually she had to spend one month in Chicago in actual hands-on training. Having passed all required examinations, she landed a job at St. Joseph's Hospital as a nurse's aide in the delivery room. Competency and fearlessness were her two hallmarks. A tireless and dedicated worker, she was an asset to my practice. She had one drawback. No one loved to cook more than Aunt Alice. Every day she would make lunch in the office's kitchenette. The lunch was always a variation on an Italian dish. In a short time, the office carried a strong odor of a pizza parlor. I mentioned this to her as diplomatically as I could. She quit in a huff, leaving me high and dry that day. Her departure precipitated the need for a professional medical assistant.

Several young ladies applied for the job, all graduates of the local business schools. They came with credentials and certificates, eager to demonstrate their proficiency in typing and taking dictation. Each one was given a medical record to transcribe on the typewriter and then a ten-minute dictation on a history and physical examination of the patient with medical terminology. They were asked to take this in shorthand and then to type it. A flawless document was issued by a young lady named Doris Sweigart. I hired her on the spot at fifty dollars a week, with no benefits except paid vacations. Doris was to prove invaluable during the next ten years of my practice. She was an exceptional, talented, and kind young lady.

In medical school, one rarely gets to see the common infectious diseases of childhood, measles, mumps, and chicken pox. The majority of these diseases are treated at home. Only very serious complications resulting from any of these common disorders are ever seen in a university hospital.

During the winter of 1959, I was called late one afternoon to see an acutely ill child with a "rash." This was a young family who lived on a farm about five miles from the office. The parents were in their late twenties, and they had three children, two boys and a girl. The sick child was a six-year-old boy who was attending first grade. He came down with a fever and runny nose three days before the parents called me to see him. The little fellow looked miserably sick. He had persisting cough and runny nose and swollen red eyes, and there was a maculopapular rash on his face, arms, and chest. Since I had never seen measles, I wasn't certain, but it certainly had all the signs and symptoms associated with measles, also known as rubella.

The grandmother was sitting in a rocking chair near the little fellow's bed, watching me carefully, as this was my first contact with this family. I asked the grandmother what she thought the little boy had, and she replied affirmatively, "Why, it's the measles, Doctor."

I agreed with her and said that we would treat it symptomatically. In those days, we still gave aspirin for viral infections, used cold cloths on the forehead to reduce fever, and generously applied tender loving care. I asked the grandmother how many cases of measles she had seen. She replied that as far as she could remember, there had been at least sixteen cases in her immediate family since she was a young girl. Armed with this knowledge, and knowing that measles can be extremely infectious, I anticipated more cases in the next week. I told the family that I wanted to come back and see little Ricky every day but that I would not charge them for more than one housecall. I did this so that I could observe and learn the course of the illness over the next week.

Returning to the office, I pulled out my textbook on pediatrics and studied childhood illnesses associated with maculopapular rashes. It was a good thing, because in the next four weeks, I would see seventy-two cases of measles. During my second visit to examine Ricky, the little sister began to show all the signs of coming down with measles, and sure enough, in two days, she had the rash. By the end of that week, having visited every day, I was thoroughly familiar with the clinical course of the disease. Now I was able to follow the signs and symptoms from the earliest stage to completion.

One early rainy morning during the epidemic, I was called to see three children in the Schlappich family, all of whom had measles. The oldest child, Dennis, was the first one to come down with the disease, followed by his sister, Donna, and younger brother, Barry. I told Mrs. Schlappich that I would come back in two days to see the children but that she should call me if there was any change. On my revisit, the younger boy and girl had a reduction of their fever and generally were feeling better. Dennis, on the other hand, complained of a headache and feeling sick in the stomach. We continued him on aspirin and a liquid diet.

The next morning, the mother called to tell me she thought he was having a convulsion. I rushed over to their home and saw that little Dennis was comatose. I told the parents that he needed to be in the hospital immediately. I suspected that he had a very serious complication from the measles, most likely measles encephalitis, an infection affecting the brain. Measles encephalitis is a rare complication, occurring only once in a thousand cases.

In the hospital, I had Dennis seen by our pediatrician, Dr. Harvey Leinbach, who confirmed the diagnosis of measles encephalitis. We would start gamma globulin injections, the only known therapy. The hospital pharmacy rapidly ran out of gamma globulin, and we had to get some from Philadelphia.

Of the many cases of measles in the county that year, Dennis had the only case of encephalitis. He did not respond to treatment and remained comatose, week after week. His mother, Blanche, was at his side every day, her face a study in love and deep concern. I explained to her that it was not likely he would die, since most deaths associated with measles encephalitis occur in the first week or two. His arms and legs began to show early contracture, shortening of the muscles that causes the limbs to flex, and it was recommended by the orthopedic group to splint them in extension (the arms straight out) to prevent permanent contracture. We did this for a few weeks, but it seemed to have an adverse effect on him, in that he became more agitated, even though he remained deep in a coma. I ordered it to be discontinued. It was often difficult for me to get to the hospital with the increased number of patients coming into the office and the inordinate number of housecalls before and after office hours.

I admitted an elderly man with bilateral pneumonia late one evening, about the thirty-fifth day that Dennis was in coma, and after I had completed the admission records and written out the treatment, I went over to the pediatric ward to visit Dennis. Except for a few night lights, the ward was dark. I pulled a chair next to his bed and looked at him in the dim light. He seemed so helpless, and so little in that pediatric bed, that I felt an overwhelming desire to pick him up and hold him, just to let him know that other humans were there to help. I whispered to him:

"We are here, Dennis. We love you. Hang on, child, please hang on!"

This is exactly how Blanche must have felt every time she came down to the hospital and sat by his side. I had read everything on measles encephalitis that was in the hospital library, and unfortunately, it was not very much, and not hopeful. Dennis had been in a coma so long, with a very high temperature in the beginning. I was certain he was going to have neurological damage—to what extent, there was no way of telling until he was conscious again. It is very rare that the brain undergoes severe inflammation, or trauma, without having serious side effects, called *sequelae*, or things following infection. In most cases, childhood measles is viewed as a trivial disease, and certainly, the great majority of children heal without incident. But unfortunately, that is not always the case.

It will surprise most people to know that during the last century and a half, over two hundred million people have died worldwide from measles. That is at least 1.3 million people every year. It is like having more than half of the population die in a city the size of Philadelphia. In 1960, that was over two million people, wiped out every year. This truly was a disease that victimized the poor and the weak. It would not be until 1963 that an effective measles vaccine would be developed.

Six weeks after the measles epidemic started, it began to diminish. Fewer and fewer cases appeared each week so that by the end of February, I saw my last case for the year. There were a few other complications, relatively minor compared to Dennis's situation, a few ear infections, one case of pneumonia, and a persistent conjunctivitis, all of which responded well to antibiotics. Each day as I made hospital rounds, I would stop to see Dennis and observed no visible changes. I told Blanche as long as he was alive, there was hope that he would recover.

On the morning of the forty-fifth day, Dennis woke up. He looked around the ward, very confused. The charge nurse saw him sitting up, and as she approached him, he said these wonderful words, "Where's my mom?"

All of the nurses on pediatric service that day were extremely happy, for they had witnessed a miracle. I know the skeptics would have a number of other natural explanations for this outcome, but for Blanche and myself, this was unquestionably the Hand of God. I know the exhausted mother had stormed heaven night and day with prayers to save her little boy, and God answered her prayers.

Dennis physically made a full recovery, but he suffered severe neurological damage. While he was able to walk and retained motor skills, his capacity to learn was limited. He would never be able to advance intellectually beyond six years old. As I write these lines, Dennis has just turned sixty. He carved out a reliable door-to-door business for himself over the years, out in the community every day, doing yard work and delivering circulars. He is well-loved by this town. Dennis's life has been one of absolute innocence. At the post office recently, he greeted me with recognition and offered the sweet, winning smile I remembered seeing the day he woke up.

By 1963, the practice had outgrown the small office building in Bernville. I decided to build a new office outside Bernville on the edge of my property that bordered on Route 183. My patients were split as to what they thought about the new building. Most of the older people, who were able to walk to the office, were strongly against it. The younger people, who had automobiles, were strongly in favor of it. My need for more space to accommodate my growing patient population mandated that I do it. We moved into the new office just before Easter, 1964. The office, a two-story building, had a complete physical therapy facility on the first floor. The reception area and waiting room, two consultation rooms, four treatment rooms, the clinical laboratory, and pharmacy were located on the second floor. My staff had grown to include an additional medical secretary, a full-time registered nurse, a full-time physical therapist, and a part-time laboratory technician, who worked in the evening. Dr. Robert Donovan, a classmate at Penn Med, joined me for a time in 1965. We then added two more registered nurses and increased our office hours.

Serving a rural community as a general practitioner, I was caught up in the routine of seasonal farming activities, the spring plowing, the planting of corn, making hay, and the most exciting part, the harvesting of the crop. The joy and associated problems of each one of these activities often depends on the weather. One clear crisp fall day during the corn harvest, I had just started my afternoon office hours shortly after lunch with a full waiting room. The receptionist ran to get me in the treatment room. Even though she was well trained, she was in a panic and blurted out, "Doctor, Clarence Luckenbill is on the phone, and he says his boy just lost his arm in a corn picker!"

I raced to the phone to ask Clarence what happened.

"Doc, it's awful!" Clarence said. "Philip got his jacket sleeve caught in the power takeoff, and it tore off his arm. Can you come up?"

"What part of the arm is torn off, the shoulder or the elbow?"

"It's the elbow, Doc."

"Is the arm bleeding a lot, Clarence?"

"No, Doc, it's just kind of oozing."

I had to think fast. This was not something for which I was trained. I had never anticipated an accident of this magnitude happening, but here it was, and I was the doctor.

"Clarence, wrap the stump in a clean towel, and put the severed arm on ice in a plastic container, a big dishwashing tub would be fine. I will meet you and your son on the Shartlesville-Bernville Road. Drive safely."

I told my staff to take care of as many patients as they could. I did not know exactly when I would be back, but I would be in touch with them. I asked Gloria, my head nurse, to call the hospital Emergency and request two surgeons, Dr. James Morrissey, the most experienced and skilled orthopedic surgeon in the county, and Dr. Arnold Van Davis, a general surgeon with considerable experience in vascular repair. I asked her to see if these two surgeons were available to stand by in Emergency.

I met Clarence and Philip in their pickup truck at the designated intersection. We both pulled into the Stoudt yard nearby. I jumped out, ran over to the truck, and looked at Philip's arm. It was not bleeding. The major arteries had contracted, and only capillary oozing was present. The severed arm was well packed in ice cubes. I assured Philip and Clarence that we were going to try to reattach this arm. The only attached severed arm in the history of surgery was done in Boston the previous year on a teenager who lost his arm at the shoulder in a train accident. A team of surgeons were able to attach this arm successfully, and he was now having some function.

When we arrived at Emergency, the surgeons were waiting. They examined the arm and concluded it would be possible to reattach it. While Clarence was sent to the admission office to take care of the paperwork, Philip was moved directly to the OR. I decided to stay with Philip during the surgery, because he was only eight years old and a very frightened little boy. We discussed possible outcomes of an attempt to reattach this arm as we prepared for surgery in the scrub-up room. Jim was mainly concerned about postoperative infection. When I mentioned the accident happened in a cornfield, they both expressed grave concern.

Cornfields are notorious for harboring a type of bacteria known as *Clostridium perfringens,* which is responsible for a serious condition known as gas gangrene. Clostridium is what we call an anaerobic organism that prefers to live in an atmosphere without oxygen, or very low oxygen levels. Once a wound was closed, the bacteria would begin to metabolize and grow. If such an infection should appear, no effective treatment existed to contain it.

After the wound had been thoroughly cleansed and examined, the articulation of the lower limb to the upper limb began by placing the bones of the lower arm in the exact position with the bone in the upper arm. I do not recall the details of much of the surgery, as it has been over fifty years since it happened. My role was to assist the two surgeons however they needed me. After the bones had been joined, the next step was to join the two ends of the brachial artery. The torn section was just above the point at which the brachial artery split into the ulnar artery and the radial artery in the lower arm. Van stitched the two ends of the severed artery together. The difficult step of joining the capsules, the ends of the upper and lower arm, was addressed by Jim. The capsules had been badly torn. Van located the torn ends of three nerves, the radial nerve, the medial nerve, and the ulnar. He was able to join the radial and medial nerves, but not the ulnar nerve. Jim examined the badly torn muscles carefully prior to reattaching them. The rotary motion of the corn picker's power takeoff had twisted off the lower arm. Jim carefully trimmed the muscles and then secured these muscles to their attachment sites. Finally, the skin was closed, drains inserted into the wound, and the joint immobilized. The operation had taken more than three hours. We were all exhausted.

We wrote postoperative orders and made an assessment of what the chances were for the arm to take hold and reestablish circulation, and then for the joint to heal. The consensus was that Philip had less than a fifty-fifty chance at best. There was no way to determine whether the blood circulation was reaching the hand and that the anastomosis, the joining of the artery, was successful. I thought that if we had a very sensitive method of measuring the heat in the finger, we would have some indication of how much circulation was being supplied to the lower arm. A medical instrument to do this did not exist. I turned to Western

Electric, a local electronic manufacturing company, for help. The plant manager offered to discuss it with his engineers and get back to me in the morning.

There were many patients yet to be seen before my day was done, so I headed back to my office. There were twenty patients waiting for me. It was well after midnight when we finished with the last patient. I did not sleep well that night. I thought about Phil, his ordeal, and what the outcome would be. I arose early in the morning and went directly to the hospital.

Overnight, the engineers at Western Electric had developed a sensitive heat-measuring instrument. They brought it to the hospital and instructed me how to use it. We attached the thermocouple to Philip's finger. To our delight, we were able to detect a slight rise in skin temperature over room temperature. The nurses were instructed to take temperature readings every hour and to record them on the chart. They were to call me if at any time the temperature fell below room temperature. Jim and Van were pleased that we were getting circulation into the hand area but remained cautious about the eventual outcome.

The boy had two and a half strikes against him because of the nature of the wound. Gas gangrene is a notorious infection, which accompanies traumatic wounds associated with crushed muscle and damaged blood vessels. We had to be vigilant, because the symptoms of gas gangrene generally do not appear until the infection reaches a dangerous zone, and then it progresses rapidly. The second day, everything seemed to be going well. The finger temperature had increased half a degree. Philip felt good, his spirits had improved, and his appetite was returning. We had put him on penicillin antibiotic therapy, hoping that would help to offset bacterial infection. I did not have a good feeling that night when I finished office hours. There was something about the wound—perhaps the color of the edges of the wound—that told me all was not well.

I arose early in the morning and went to the hospital to check Philip. Arriving there about 6:00 a.m., I put on sterile gloves and felt the edges of the wound. To my horror, crepitus, a crackling feeling of gas under the skin, was present. This was an unmistakable sign that gas gangrene had started. Gas gangrene spreads very rapidly. The outcome is fatal in greater than 25 percent of patients. I immediately called Dr. Morrissey and Dr. Davis to inform them of my findings. They came to Philip's room before their scheduled surgeries at seven o'clock. We collectively decided the only thing we could possibly do to save this boy's life was to remove the attached lower arm. I called Clarence, Phillip's father, to let him know the situation. I explained that if we tried to save the arm, we ran a high risk of the gangrene spreading and that we could lose the boy.

Clarence broke into tears and said, "Save the boy, Doc. Please save the boy!"

Philip's surgery was given high priority. He was moved almost immediately to the OR where the attached arm was removed and the infection cleaned. As they closed the wound, Dr. Morrissey noticed that the end of the *coracobrachialis* muscle was of a grayish color. He told Van about this and that he wanted to explore this muscle to make sure that it did not contain Clostridium. Dissecting the muscle to the shoulder, he found that the whole muscle was rotten with Clostridium. They removed the muscle. The wound was left open until the infection had cleared. Had it not been for Dr. Morrissey's experience and keen observation, the wound would have been closed and Phillip would surely have died.

Phil made a rapid recovery following the surgery and was home within ten days. He faced a new life, with many difficult adjustments. He would need a considerable amount of training in order to function with one arm, and he would need to make quite a few social adjustments. After several weeks, I observed that Philip was becoming depressed and not adjusting well to the situation. After visiting Philip at the farm, I recalled another patient, a veteran who had lost his arm in the invasion of Normandy in World War II. Sodoy, a young farmer, had made many adjustments to the rigors of farming with one arm. I knew that Sodoy had undergone periods of depression, which I believed were related to his disability. I called Sodoy to ask him if he would come to see me to discuss the possibility of helping Philip. He seemed to hesitate at first. As he listened, he was moved by this little boy's story of survival. Sodoy agreed to come and said he would be at my office within an hour. After our discussion, he said he agreed to help Philip, because he knew how difficult it had been to try to make his way in our society with only one arm. His generosity toward the boy was returned to him in kind. Through helping Philip, the wounded soldier gained a new outlook on his own life. Over the years, Sodoy and Philip became and remained great friends.

It is many years now since Philip had his accident. He has married, raised several children, and continues to farm. Looking back on this incident, I thank God for everyone who was critical to saving his life.

Jake Lesher and I sat on his porch watching the traffic go by. Jake was wonderstruck that there were three cars on Main Street at one time that evening.

"Ach my, Doc, I have never seen more than two cars at one time on Main Street, and that was usually on a parade day!"

We were well into a plate of Lepp raisin cookies when Jake's nephew, a salesman of fine cutlery, stopped by the porch and informed Jake that he was making a sales trip early next week to New York City.

"Uncle Jake, do you want to go with?"

Jake had never been out of Berks County. In his younger years, he traveled to Reading every Saturday to market his homegrown produce, but otherwise, he'd never made a longer trip than fifteen miles. He had never seen the Philadelphia historical sites in Pennsylvania's largest city, just eighty miles away. Jake accepted the invitation eagerly and told his nephew he would be "ready to go over" any time.

I saw Jake at the end of the following week. He was still giddy with excitement as he told me about this trip. He had already been telling stories for days at the Agway and Burkey's and the post office about the sights of the city. I asked Jake what impressed him most about New York. Without a moment's hesitation, he looked at me wide-eyed and said, "Vhy, do you know, Doctor, you can buy a soft pretzel on every corner of every street! And that ain't just on Saturday, but every day!"

Jake was referring to Penn Street in Reading, where only one street vendor sold soft pretzels, and this occurred only on Saturday. Lovers of soft pretzels had to wait week to week to enjoy their favorite doughy treat. In the late fifties, Reading was the hard pretzel capital of the world, but only one shop offered soft pretzels.

Jake was a pretzel fan. "You know, Doctor, vhy you can even get mustard on your pretzel and it doesn't cost a penny more. They even sell soda pop from these little carts, and hot dogs, too!" He continued excitedly describing the food conveniences of New York, until finally he came to marvel about the buildings.

"I never saw such tall buildings! Geezumpete, you can't even see the top of those buildings from the street unless you lay down on the sidewalk!" I knew he would not make such a statement unless, yes, Jake had gone supine on the sidewalk, staring up at the buildings while people walked all around him. He spoke endlessly about the traffic, about the policeman on horseback, and about the people rushing on the street. He was amazed that on a weekday, every street he saw was "as busy as Penn Street on a Saturday afternoon, even all the restaurants were crowded, all day long!"

He wanted to know if I had ever been to New York, and why I had to go there. I explained I went there frequently for medical meetings and occasionally to shop. Overwhelmed that such a magnanimous event as a day in New York could happen more than once in a lifetime, Jake shook his head and expressed the all-occasion sentiment of Bernville at times of great wonderment.

"Aye, yiiii, yiiii!"

A man who identified himself as Mike called about his brother who was very inebriated, in the cow stable with a pistol and would not come out. His brother, Charlie, had been in the stable for two days, severely depressed and very hostile. The family was of Slavic background. I knew that family well. Charlie had been a patient for many years.

The mother had been killed a month earlier in a tractor accident. At eighty years old, she was trying to change a front tire on a John Deere tractor when the jack slipped and the front of the tractor fell, impaling her on the jack. She must have died instantly. When I arrived, some thirty minutes later, she had been dead for some time. The call I received was from her son Mike in Philadelphia.

Charlie was a bachelor, handsome and very intelligent. He was a hardworking and ambitious young man. Charlie was dedicated to building up his family's dairy farm, using the latest scientific methods in every aspect of farming. His farm was his life. We had many discussions not only about farming, but also about the difficulty of being accepted in the Pennsylvania Dutch community when you are not of German descent. He felt this more acutely than I did, probably because he interacted more closely with the established farming community. I'm sure he was ostracized by many local people. The Pennsylvania Dutch were very slow to accept "outsiders," which meant you were neither German nor a Protestant.

I could not understand what in the world happened that would drive Charlie to these desperate measures. I told Mike I would go right away to see what the problem was. It was around 6:30 a.m. I told Joanne I would be back shortly to have breakfast. Little did I realize what I was getting into.

When I arrived at the farm, I drove directly to the cow barn, parked my car, and walked over to the large sliding doors to go into the barn to look for Charlie. As I approached the barn, I heard a gunshot. It sounded like a .38 as it whizzed over my head.

I hit the deck as fast as I could. My military training had taught me that this was the safest thing to do when someone fires at you. I called to Charlie, but I got no answer. I crawled back to my car and drove behind the silo, which would protect me from any more bullets. This was not a situation I could handle alone. I called the State Police with the radiotelephone in my car. I told the sergeant that I had a very disturbed, drunken adult holed up in a cow stable with a pistol that sounded like a .38 caliber. I gave him directions to the farm. He told me to stay put. A team of officers would be there in less than thirty minutes, the time it would take to drive the thirteen miles from the Hamburg state police barracks. I called Joanne next to let her know I would not be home for breakfast, but I didn't tell her what the situation was.

As I waited for the state police, I could hear Charlie talking in the barn, cursing and shouting. I wondered what extreme circumstances drove him to this state. This behavior was so unlike him. Six well-armed state police arrived. I explained what little I knew of the situation. I told them that Charlie was a docile, salt-of-the-earth, intelligent person and that this behavior was beyond anything I could account for. I did not know what part of the barn he was in, but I guessed that he was in the area where the cows were, known as the milking parlor. The officers discussed their strategy for a few minutes and then told me to stay in the car.

They divided into groups of three and went cautiously into the barn. I expected to hear shots ring out and an exchange of fire, but there was none. Charlie battled with all six officers, and quite a battle it must have been. Two of the officers ended up with lacerations that had to be repaired later in my office, and two others had badly torn uniforms. They emerged with Charlie handcuffed. They dragged him over to the squad car. One of the officers approached me and said they were taking him to jail.

"Officer," I explained, "I am the physician for Berks County Prison, and I think he would do better at Wernersville State Hospital. He is mentally ill, and he needs to be helped. We can take him there, and I can sign him in."

They thought for a while and then agreed. I called the State Hospital to let them know we were coming and described the patient we wanted to admit. Three of the police took Charlie to the State Hospital, while I drove to my office to treat the other two officers who had been hurt. They both had lacerations, one on the hand and the other on the face. The officers were impressed by how strong Charlie was and what a terrific fight he put up. After they left, I headed for the State Hospital to see Charlie. He was still drunk and sullen. I told the attending physician that I wanted to see Charlie when he had sobered up and was able to talk with me. I explained that his behavior that morning was completely out of character for Charlie, who was widely read and interested in many things. Three days later, the doctor called to say that Charlie was ready to speak with me.

Charlie's heavily guarded room was in the criminal section. He was the most dejected and desolate person I had ever seen. The institutional furniture was sparse and heavy, a lifeless contrast to the comforting colors of the home life from which he had been forcibly removed just days ago. The thin hospital pajamas and robe hung on his frame like hand-me-downs, his eyes sunken into his once-handsome face. He was unrecognizable, including the belligerent expression he attempted when I entered the room.

"How are you, Charlie?" I asked.

"Terrible, Doctor. It's the end of the world for me. I have nothing to live for, no place to go—just awful . . ." Then he began to sob.

I sat down beside him and put my hand on his shoulder.

"Can you tell me what happened, Charlie?"

An angry memory flashed in his eyes, but that spark just as quickly faded to sadness and despair.

"I have lost everything I've worked for over the last twenty years," he said. "My mother and father promised me that if I stayed and worked the farm, they would give it to me as a reward for my service to them. I agreed to stay and promised to share with my brother and sister if the farm was ever sold. I spent my whole life making the farm profitable. My work has allowed us to keep the farm and supported my parents. Three days ago, I found out that my mother had willed the farm to my sister. My brother Mike and I were to get nothing. I tried to make a deal with my sister to remain on the farm and to work it. She intended to sell it as soon as she could. Since everything was in my parents' names, I could do nothing. I spoke with a lawyer who told me I had no recourse to the law. Now I am destitute and feel betrayed."

"Charlie, that is absolutely awful," I said, meaning it. "I know how hard you worked and how much effort you put into that farm. I just can't believe your mother and sister would do that to you!" I said, with genuine astonishment.

"It's true, Doctor, I can't believe it. I don't know what I am going to do. What can I do?"

I struggled to find the words to console him. "You are a very intelligent man, Charlie. You have suffered a great loss and a crushing disappointment, but it's not the end of the world for you. I have never known you to be a religious man, but I suggest at this difficult time, you pray to God for guidance. Your family cannot take your intelligence and your spirit from you. To be sure, seeing your life's work lost by a stroke of a pen is devastating. It's not easy to begin over, but you did this once and you can do it again. Terrible things can happen to us for reasons we don't understand. I believe every crisis presents new opportunities. We only see the bad at first, but eventually, some good things can result from a disaster. I know you find it hard to accept any of this right now. Stay here, in the hospital until you feel better. Try to look for a positive that can come from this. And, Charlie, trust in God."

I knew I had to leave him in the care of the psychiatrists. I stood up to leave, reached for his hand, and told him, "Charlie, I consider you a friend, and I will be here when you need me." He held on for a minute and then fell on his cot and sobbed.

Charlie was a vigorous, productive man whose life was ruined by broken promises and a greedy, ungrateful sister. I never saw him again. Years later, I heard that he moved to West Virginia and died at the age of fifty-seven.

This story reminds me that nothing is certain in life. How a single almost insignificant incident can destroy a life, a family, even a country!

I was making a housecall to Rehrersburg one morning. On the main road into town, a stupendous barn fire was blazing. Two volunteer fire companies fighting the fire had no hope of controlling the inferno. Tons of hay were set ablaze. The huge barn was consumed in a few minutes. I pulled over to see if anyone was hurt and found to my relief that no life was lost and no one was injured. An electrical failure of a makeshift wiring attempt by the farmer caused the fire. In an effort to save a few hundred dollars, he had lost tens of thousands and jeopardized the entire neighboring community. How many times are we told nothing in life is certain, that we have what we have only for the moment? So few of us understand or appreciate that simple fact. I watched the framework collapse, smoke billowing as firemen aimed their hoses at the black and charred timbers. Most likely the farmer had insurance and would rebuild his barn. Everything would return to the way it was, as if nothing had happened. The people of the town would have something to talk about for a few days, a bit of excitement, something to perk up their humdrum lives. Few, if any, would reflect on the impermanence of things. What keeps us from appreciating how precious our lives and our loved ones are? We should treasure every moment that we have. I don't know why this fundamental understanding is so elusive.

Bernville is about eight miles or so from the little town of Mohrsville, accessible by a winding, treacherous road, often impassable in the winter. Late one evening, I received a call from a frantic young mother that she feared her two-year-old son was dying. He was being treated for pneumonia and was apparently not responding. I assured her I would be there as quickly as possible. We had seen the last patient and were finishing up with the paperwork. Snow was beginning to fall, not a good sign for the trip to Mohrsville.

I found the mother crying, while the young father looked on with great anxiety. The child was moribund, gray in color, and barely breathing. I told the mother to wrap the child in a blanket. We were going to the hospital. I thought for a moment she would collapse, but her husband stood by her and took the child as she cried uncontrollably. Without wasting a moment, we moved her along into the car. She sat up front with me. Their older child and her husband sat in the backseat. The husband planned to call his parents from the hospital and arrange for them to come down. I drove as quickly as I could, instructing the mother to keep the child's head elevated so that his breathing would be somewhat eased. She kept wondering why this happened to her child. She wanted to know why the other doctor who saw her boy did not recognize the condition sooner. I tried to explain that in clinical situations, particularly with children, one set of symptoms may be interpreted by a physician as non-threatening, but within ten to twenty minutes, the situation can deteriorate. You have to make the diagnosis at the time you see the patient. Often signs and symptoms change after an examination. Doctors know this phenomenon. We are reluctant to criticize any physician who examined the patient, even an hour earlier. She claimed she understood, but I doubt that she heard what I said. She was so overwhelmed with concern for the life of her child that anything I said to her would not sink in. I tried to avoid any other questions, because her son's situation was so serious I could not say anything to make her feel better. I let her know that I would have the best chest surgeon in the county available to treat her son. I told her that doctors fully understood this condition and that we had a very effective method of treating it. She mumbled a few thankful words as she held her child close to her.

I could do nothing else but pray. I prayed that this child would survive long enough to reach the hospital. I knew that he most likely would respond very well if we just kept him alive. His breathing was extremely labored, very shallow in the atmosphere of the car. I could not get a good impression of his color, but it appeared that he was becoming more ashen gray.

I thought of a family story I'd heard. When I was two years old, I was acutely ill with a severe case of pneumonia. The physician was an older Italian gentleman, not well-versed in modern medicine. In the dead of winter, 1928, the doctor called on us every other day to treat my infected chest with mustard plasters. Mustard plasters consisted of crushed mustard seed paste placed on a hot cloth, applied to the chest area to add heat. This treatment concept was based strictly on getting more blood to the area to provide more body resources to treat the infection. It was not effective. As I became progressively worse, my grandfather, Pietro, stopped by to see me while the doctor was attending me. My grandfather, for whom I was named, informed him that I was getting worse and that he wanted a second medical opinion. The Italian doctor did not object. According to my father's account, Dr. Gerhard came into the room, looked at me, and without examining me said, "Take this boy to the hospital immediately. He is dying."

My father asked why and how he knew that without examining me. Dr. Gerhard came over to my bed and tapped me on the chest and said, "He is full of pus from here to his neck." He picked me up, wrapped me in a blanket, and carried me to his car. My dad went with him as they rushed me to the hospital and into surgery. I only remember the smell of ether, the red tube they were sticking into my chest, and a large drainage bottle beside the operating table. I made an uneventful recovery and was back on my feet in relatively short time. I remembered this story my whole life.

I was now the doctor trying to save the life of another child with pneumonia. I thought about what must have happened when I was two years old and Dr. Gerhard had saved my life. Though I had never seen a child with empyema, the same disease I had suffered, this is what this child had. I had treated two adults with it during my practice. Recalling what my father had told me about my own childhood illness made me fully realize that this was a life or death matter. I had no time to waste, and I needed a surgeon trained in thoracic diseases to help me save this child.

When we arrived at the hospital at seven o'clock, I asked the emergency nurse to order a chest film. The thoracic surgeon was on his way to the hospital. While waiting for Dr. Cohen, I went to the x-ray department to check the film and ordered that the child be taken to the OR. When I walked into the x-ray office, the radiologist said, "Peter, you have a very, very sick child here."

"Yes, George," I replied, "I know, and I have called Hal to come to the OR where the little boy is now. I'm going up there right away to make sure everything is ready when Hal arrives."

By the time Dr. Hal Cohen arrived, the child was on the table and the anesthesiologist was working on him. Hal examined the infant, confirmed the diagnosis, and went immediately to scrub and prepare for the surgery. I scrubbed to assist him in this operation. The first incision he made into the chest produced a flood of pus over the table, which he let flow, collecting it in a basin. He inserted a suction tube connected to a Wagensteen suction apparatus. We drained a fair amount of pus from his right side but did not apply suction to the left side. Cultures of the pus were taken. He was placed on an antibiotic. I was pleased his color had improved tremendously, and his breathing was a lot easier, though he still looked seriously ill. We sent him to intensive care for close monitoring that night.

After he was transferred to intensive care and I was sitting in the nurse's station reviewing the postop orders Hal had written, I thanked God that all the pieces came together and that we were able to save the boy. I turned my attention to the mother, who was sitting in the waiting area of intensive care.

Her desperate, worried look, expecting the worst possible outcome for her child, had not changed. I was able to give her the reassuring news that her child was going to be all right and that she would be able to see him in just a few more minutes. I explained that we had drained a lot of pus from his lung, making it easier for him to breathe and that we had taken cultures to find the right antibiotic. Until we had those results, we started him on another antibiotic, which we felt would be effective against the infection. As I spoke with her, the lines on her face gradually vanished, as though someone had taken a magical eraser and wiped them out. The stress had drained a great deal out of her. Now that she had hope, her whole demeanor changed. She collapsed on the chair and cried and cried with happiness. Her husband sat next to her with his arm around her, holding her hand, and stroking it with his thumb. After about five minutes, I suggested we go back to see her son, who by this time had recovered from the anesthesia. He recognized his mother immediately and feebly raised a hand to touch her. She bent over and kissed him. I could see she wanted to hug him, but she knew that was not a good idea. She was overjoyed to see her little boy breathing better and his color so improved.

I stopped to see the little boy the next morning. The surgeon had already been there. He changed some dressings and made a positive note in his chart. When I approached the little patient's bed, he looked up at me and gave me a small smile. I knew he was still plenty sick, but I was delighted to see that smile. I visited him every day during the next week until he was ready for discharge. Each day, he got stronger, was able to take food, and eventually could sit up in bed. He was so eager to get out of that bed that we had a problem keeping him down. He did find he was not quite as strong as he thought he was once he was up.

His clinical course was uneventful. He made rapid progress to full recovery. He was discharged ten days later. I suggested that his mother carry him to the car, which was really just a short distance. I recommended that he should have bed rest whenever he was tired at home. It could take as long as six weeks before his chest was completely healed.

As they walked out of the hospital, he had his little head over her shoulder. He was smiling at me. He waved good-bye with his little hand, but he said nothing. In that moment, I realized that if I did nothing else worthwhile the rest of my life, I had saved the life of a little boy and prevented a great deal of anguish to a fragile mother. It felt good to be alive, doing what I do.

I was married to an extraordinary woman, a woman whom I would not ever fully understand. Even in her youth, Joanne was a woman of immense talent in many areas, who had the capacity to love at times bordering on the infinite. My love for her became greater as each year went by. No matter how close we became, she always remained a mystery to me. I can recall so many instances when her intuition was uncanny. She had a way of assessing people's honesty and sincerity that was just short of the miraculous. She sometimes made mistakes, mistakes that I attributed to her kindness and sympathy for people, which would override her judgment now and then. As in any marriage, we had our problems, most of which can be attributed to me and my attention to medicine.

One day at lunch, I asked one of my doctor friends, who was a university professor, if he would do anything differently after thirty years of being a physician. He was a man very devoted to his family and had a handicapped, bedridden child whose need for care made it impossible for him to leave home overnight. He looked at me with an intensely serious face and replied, "I would spend more time with my family, and I am sure you would, too."

Of course, he was right.

A doctor's family is often compared to the shoemaker's son, who is shoeless while surrounded by shoes. One night, while I was watching a TV program about Dr. Paul Ehrlich and the discovery of vaccines, my son Steven came downstairs complaining of abdominal pain. Since the next morning was a school day, I assumed that this was another ruse to get out of going to school. I told him to go back to bed, that the pain would be better in the morning. He went up to bed.

In a few minutes, he was down again. He was bent over with his hand on his right side. He said, "Dad, it's not that kind of pain. This really hurts!"

I had him lie down on the sofa and examined his abdomen. To my surprise, he had all the classic signs of acute appendicitis. I called Dr. Davis and told him I was sure Steve had acute appendicitis. I arranged to meet him in the emergency room. We drove the thirteen miles to Reading Hospital and found Dr. Davis waiting when we arrived. After examining my son, he agreed on the diagnosis. We moved Steve to the OR. It is a very strange feeling to be assisting in an operation on your own child, not at all like operating on a stranger.

All went well with the surgery. I went down to see Steve in the recovery room after surgery to tell him everything was okay and that I would see him in the morning. He looked so very little and helpless lying in that recovery room. When I arrived home and told Joanne that everything went well, I could see the look of relief as a smile lit up her face. Always a Chicken Little, she was expecting the worst. Steve made an uneventful recovery. I learned from this experience to be objective about my children and their ills and to always get a second opinion.

One morning, I received a call at 5:30 from an elderly patient, Mr. Tobias. He had fallen and cracked his lip. I suggested he come to the office immediately if it was bleeding badly. He claimed the bleeding had stopped, except for a little oozing. He could wait. When I saw him at seven o'clock in the office, he looked as if he had been hit in the face with a dull hatchet. A gaping, ugly, ragged laceration extended from the middle of his nose to his lower lip.

"Good Lord, Amos, what in the world happened?" I asked.

Amos was eighty-four years old, a tall, rugged man wearing a fur hat, overalls, and an old wool topcoat. He had his work boots on, typical of those worn by Berks County farmers. He explained what happened to him.

He was up early gathering eggs. As he was crossing the lane between his house and the chicken coop, he tripped while stepping over a rutted, icy path. His face hit the frozen dirt with full force.

"You have any pain, Amos?" I asked.

"No, Doctor," he responded, "not that I can't stand."

I had never repaired a laceration of this severity on the face and told him so and that for cosmetic reasons he may choose to go to the hospital to have it repaired. He looked at me and said, "You are my doctor, and I ain't going to be in any beauty contests at eighty-four years old. Do the best job you can."

In a country practice, you are expected to do many things that you would never anticipate doing. In the city, an endless supply of specialists would handle these things for you, but it is not the case for the country doctor. Amos pretty much summarized my role. I was the surgeon.

I set to work repairing this laceration. After cleaning and anesthetizing the edges, I debrided the wound, that is, I cut away all of the dead and dirty tissue, making sure the wound was clean. I had to make sure that the edges of the lips were approximated accurately. I achieved this with 4-0 silk, very fine suture material that comes already threaded onto a surgical needle. I generously applied a solution of cocaine, which was commonly used as a short-acting topical anesthetic, to the nasal mucosa. I think this is still used in nasal surgery today. I was able to close the inner mucosa with 4-0 cat gut. Suture material made of gut is used whenever the sutures are not to be removed, and it will be absorbed by the body. It is actually made from cattle intestine, not cats. The outer laceration on the nose was closed with 4-0 silk, the same type of suture I used to approximate the lacerated lip edges. When it was all done, I gave him the necessary immunizations against tetanus. I let him know he had to come in to see me the next day, to make sure there was no infection.

Amos asked if I had a mirror, to see what he looked like after the surgery. I had not bandaged the wound, since I would have had to cover his mouth. No Pennsylvania Dutchman would stand for that, since it would preclude his eating. I had a small hand mirror in the treatment room which I gave to him. He looked at himself from different angles and then, managing a small smile, he said, "Gee whiz, Doctor, why I don't look any different than I did yesterday, except for these black whiskers you stuck in me." We both got a little laugh at that.

After Mr. Tobias left the office, I completed the record for his chart. I made a sketch of the laceration, and the repair, and noted the immunizations he had been given. When I saw him again, there were no complications and no infection. I was extremely proud of the result. Two weeks later, I removed the silk stitches and his healing was almost complete. He had a very small scar running from the top of his lip to the bottom of his left nostril. Within two years, this was no longer visible. I have always been proud of that little bit of surgery.

One evening, I had been up almost until midnight seeing patients in the office. I dragged myself to bed and fell sound asleep within a matter of a few minutes. About 2:30 a.m., the ringing of the phone awakened me. There is no more chilling sound to a physician than a telephone ringing at two or three o'clock in the morning. Groggily, I picked up the receiver. Curtis Hottenstein was on the line to tell me that his mother had fallen down a flight of steps and was lying injured at the bottom. Curtis was not a man to be easily excited. His voice on this occasion was filled with concern. This urgency caused me to dress quickly and get to his farm. Elsie, his wife, was waiting at the door when I arrived. She showed me to the stairwell, where I found Amanda, not quite ninety, in a heap of tangled nightclothes sprouting arms and legs. She was conscious, obviously in pain, and did not want to be moved in any way. I explained to her that I had to move her to examine her. She reluctantly agreed. To my relief, there were no open wounds and no apparent external bleeding. Both clavicles in the collarbone appeared to be fractured, as well as her left humerus, upper arm. Her right leg was bent at an angle indicating that she had broken her femur, thigh bone, about midway down the leg. She seemed to have a Collie's fracture of her left lower arm. The accident happened about an hour earlier when Amanda got out of bed to go to the bathroom. There were two adjacent doors, one leading to the bathroom, and the other opened on the stairwell. Amanda had chosen the wrong door, stepped headlong into space, and rolled down the steps.

I explained to Curtis and Elsie that we would have to move his mother to the hospital in an ambulance. When Amanda heard this, she turned her head to look at me and said firmly, "Stuff and nonsense! I'm not going to the hospital. I have never been in a hospital, and I'm not going now."

"Amanda, you have many broken bones which are almost impossible to treat here. I do not know if you have any internal injuries. We need x-rays, some laboratory tests, and a hospital bed to treat the fractures properly."

"If you're any kind of a doctor, you would be able to treat me without all that hospital business. When I was kicked by the cow and broke my leg here," she said, pointing to her upper right leg, "Dr. Herbein took care of it right on the farm. We didn't have x-rays then, and he didn't need them. I'm not going to the hospital."

I turned to Curtis and Elsie and said, "Let's see if we can get her upstairs in a chair."

She was lying in the corner of the landing at the bottom of the steps leading to the second floor. The steps made a right angle turn at the landing and three additional steps completed the connection to the first floor. The space was cramped. We took a wooden ladder-back chair and maneuvered it on the steps. While Elsie held the chair, Curtis and I slipped our arms under Amanda's buttocks, held her around the shoulders and back, and lifted her high enough to allow Elsie to put the chair under her. Though this caused her a great deal of pain, I knew of no other way to get her up the steps. Once she was in the chair, I attempted to straighten her leg to reduce the fracture, but there was so much muscle spasm I could not achieve a reduction. Curtis exchanged places with Elsie while I took the bottom legs of the chair. We carried Amanda up the steps.

In the meantime, Elsie had taken the covers off her mother-in-law's bed and arranged her pillows to keep her head high. We had to lift Amanda off the chair while Elsie guided the broken leg first, and then the good leg, onto the bed. Despite the intense pain, Amanda did not cry out. Before we moved her, I considered giving her some Demerol™ to help her pain, but I was not certain whether or not she had a head injury. Even though she was conscious and rational, I wanted to do a more thorough neurological exam once I had her safely in bed.

Now came some real problems. I had no orthopedic equipment in my medical bag. I had to go to the hospital to get the necessary supplies. Obtaining equipment from the hospital in the early morning from the Cast Room would be just short of a miracle. A rigorous procedure was required to get a single bandage from the Cast Room, most of which related to the cost of whatever you were asking for. I pleaded with the night supervisor to no avail. Finally, I had to call the medical director to get his permission. He was not happy about being awakened in the wee hours of the morning for material to take care of her fractures, but he did give me permission. I secured the necessary equipment, signed pages and pages of records, and headed back to the farm to treat Amanda.

The first thing I did was to give Amanda an injection of Demerol™, which allowed her to sleep without pain and made it somewhat less uncomfortable for her as I went about trying to reduce her fractures. I examined her abdomen and her chest. Except for a few contusions on the left part of her chest, there were no fractured ribs, and no evidence of any abdominal injuries. My first task was to get the femur, the thigh bone, into traction. I used a system known as the Bucks extension. This is a device that pulls the lower leg with a series of weights in an endeavor to reduce and hold the fracture in place. With the sedation and ten to twenty minutes of traction on the leg, I was able to reduce the fractured femur. I next used a figure-eight bandage to treat the bilateral fractured clavicles. I applied a sling to treat the fractured humerus and an ace bandage to the hand and wrist for the Collies fracture, which I realized was not actually a true Collies fracture but most likely a break of the head of the radius. Without an x-ray, I could not really tell.

Curtis and Elsie left around 5:30 a.m. to do the milking. It took me until after 6:30 to finish everything. Amanda slept quietly. Occasionally, she would try to move and would moan. From a practical point of view, I was concerned about how she was going to urinate and how we would take care of her bowels. I didn't think that Elsie would be capable of handling this, so I planned to have one of my nurses insert a Foley catheter the next day. I knew Amanda would object to this vehemently, but there wasn't any other way. I called Joanne, told her I would not be home for least another hour, and explained what had happened.

Elsie came in and started to make breakfast. She said I should stay for breakfast so that I could explain what the next steps were. I was happy to do this. Not only was I very hungry, but Elsie was a wonderful cook. At breakfast, I explained that we needed to get some fluid into Amanda and some food. I checked later that day and found she had taken only a few teaspoons of ginger ale. That was all I needed to know to start intravenous fluids.

The intravenous fluid process in the hospital is so routine that no one ever considers all the work that goes into it. The calculations of intake and output, total body needs for fluid, kidney function, nutrition, and a host of other things all have to be considered. When I mentioned this to Curtis and Elsie, they almost despaired. Elsie said she would do the best she could. After our office hours that day, I made rounds at the hospital and then went down to the hospital pharmacy to get the fluids. I had a good rapport with the pharmacist and who let me purchase whatever I needed without a huge amount of paperwork. Returning to the farm that evening, I had two boxes of intravenous fluids and ten IV administration kits.

I set up 5 percent glucose and water as her initial IV, carefully showing the process to Elsie and making sure that she understood the procedure. I told her she need not worry about putting the needle in the vein. I would take care of that. If she needed any help at any time, she just had to give me a call. She was particularly interested in how to regulate the drip rate, which I explained carefully. I told her she would probably have to set her alarm clock for the next bottle. All in all, she seemed confident that she could handle it. I would have to make at least two housecalls every day to check on the intravenous feedings and Amanda's general status. One of my nurses stopped by once a day to see what nursing care she needed. This was before the time of Medicare, so we did not charge for all of our services. Knowing Amanda's care and treatment would extend for eight weeks or more, I had to arrange my schedule in order to accommodate her needs.

After a week, Curtis called and said he wanted to see me. Elsie was having a devil of a time trying to keep up with the intravenous feedings, the care of Amanda, the housekeeping, and the milking. We sat at the table having a cup of coffee while I explained the options to them. The first was to move Amanda to the hospital, but we knew that she would object to that very strongly. The second was to hire a full-time nurse to care for her. Though Curtis could have afforded this service, he chose not to hire a nurse, because his mother would object to spending the money. The third option was to discontinue the intravenous feedings altogether. I explained to Curtis and Elsie the consequences of this action. Unless Amanda was able to take fluids and nourishment by mouth, she would not live longer than a week. I explained the body's need for fluids, the role of the kidneys, and how dehydration could so damage the body that she would die. Elsie explained that continuing at this pace would kill her, because she herself had early congestive heart failure. I agreed that we could not expect her to endanger herself in caring for Amanda. Curtis asked if there was a chance that she could survive on small quantities of fluid by mouth. I told him she would need to take at least a quart of liquid every day and a certain number of calories. Curtis was very concerned for his wife as well as for his mother. He was quiet for a while and then told me to stop the IVs. He decided to give his mother frequent liquids by mouth. He was well aware of the risk he was taking, but he felt confident that his mother's constitution was strong enough to survive this ordeal. I went up to her room and discontinued the intravenous feedings. I explained to Amanda how important it was that she try to take as much fluid by mouth as she could. At the time, she was taking one or two tablespoons of ginger ale, two to three times a day. That was hardly enough to keep her alive. I told Curtis to give me a call if there was a change, otherwise I would see her again in three days. I fully expected her not to survive.

Three days later, after hospital rounds in the morning, I called Curtis to check on Amanda. He said she was taking more fluids and asking for solid food. I arranged to stop on the way home from the hospital to check on her. When I arrived, she was sitting in bed eating a bowl of oatmeal. She wanted me to remove the ace bandage that I put on her shoulders to reduce the fractured clavicles. I explained that it was too early and that I was planning to replace them. She reluctantly agreed to wear them another week, but then she wanted to be done with it.

When I returned in a week, she had removed the ace bandages herself, along with the support on her hand that I had applied to treat the fractured radius. I knew it was useless to make a fuss. After all, it was her life, her clavicles, and her radius. Amanda was the toughest old bird I ever treated. I planned to see her just once a week, to make sure that her fractured arm and fractured leg were still doing well. Far from dying from her injuries, Amanda recovered her mobility and lost none of her steely stubbornness. She would be the very last patient I treated, ahead many years hence and well past her one hundredth birthday.

The homebound treatment of Amanda had taken its toll on me. I was exhausted. I suggested to Joanne we should get away for at least a weekend. She made arrangements for my mother to take care of the children. The next morning, we were on our way for a few days of relaxation. We went to King of Prussia, about an hour away where there was an excellent bookstore, a fine bakery known as the Sticky Bun Shop, and lots of antique stores. I slept soundly for the first time in weeks. Having time to spend with Joanne was indescribably delightful. I recalled a little episode of St. John the Evangelist. One day as he stood at a well, he was playing with a bird.

One of his disciples took him to task, saying, "Is it not beyond your dignity to be standing here playing with a bird?"

St. John answered him, "Do you see those soldiers standing in front of the tavern?"

"Yes," came the reply.

"Do you notice that they have their bow strings unslung?"

When the disciple answered that he did notice it, St. John then asked him why the soldiers did not have their bows under tension. The disciple answered that if the bows were always under tension, they would lose their strength and become useless.

St. John then said to him, "This is what I am doing now. I am unslinging my bow."

Every physician must unsling his bow from time to time.

CHAPTER 9

Shades of the Edge People

During my seminary days, one of the privileges of being an upperclassman was to go on the home missions. At no time were prep students from the Minor House allowed to go into the residence of the upperclassmen, known as the Major House, without permission from the dean of the Minor House, but on holidays, we prep students did have a chance to mingle. The home missions were in the mountains mainly at the junction of Arkansas and Missouri, though there were other areas in Arkansas that were considered mission areas. I was particularly intrigued by the tales told by fellow seminarians who were on the missions in the Ozark Mountains.

A history of trust had been established among the backwoods people for the priests to visit. The families that we essentially infiltrated to bring spiritual education were remotely situated away from the towns. The people lived within highly independent, self-sufficient communities, a society unto themselves. So far removed were they that the seminarians called them "the edge people." The children had never seen an electric light or heard a radio. They did not know what a bathroom was and had never seen a flush toilet or shower, or refrigerator. All of the stoves were woodstoves, lighting was with kerosene, and food preservation was either by desiccation, salting, or root cellars.

One of the seminarians, Don, explained that these people were not fully integrated into the modern life of nearby Little Rock, or even the small towns they could reach on foot. They grew or hunted most of what they ate. As such, they lived on the fringes of society, or as the seminarians perceived it, on the edge. It is no wonder that when I first drove on the road to visit a patient known to the locals as the *Hundzgranny*, I felt I was going back into time. It called to mind the days before I was a doctor . . . a teenager wearing a cassock, hearing the seminary tales of the Edge People.

Harold Cypress had been a patient of mine for at least ten years, perhaps even longer. I never saw him sober or bathed. He was one of the most unkempt individuals I had ever known. Only when he fractured several ribs, did I have the opportunity to remedy his awful hygiene. I seized the chance to clean him up and finally get him into a shower.

"Now, Cy," I approached the subject with caution, "the first thing you need to do, before we can treat those broken ribs, is to get some moist heat on them and then massage the area over your chest."

"How the hell do I do that?" he barked.

"I know your son has a shower. What I suggest is that you set the water temperature so it's somewhere between tepid and comfortably hot, then get under it. Use soap as a lubricant. Rub it all over your chest and carefully massage the area where you have pain. Then let the water flow over you for at least five to eight minutes. After you dry off, have your son put this six-inch ace bandage around your chest. Come in to the office in the morning, and we will fit you with the proper rib belt."

The thought of being that close to soap and water made him very upset. He continued to swear all the time that he was leaving the office with his son. Cy never spoke more than three words without some horrible expletive to emphasize his statement.

At nine o'clock the next morning, he arrived. It marked the first time I was aware that he actually had white skin. He let out a stream of vulgarities and damnations that would embarrass a platoon of seasoned Marines. (I have not included them here.)

"That was the dumbest damn foolish thing anybody ever told me to do! Why, Doc, that water beating down on my head gave me such a headache I had to have two or three drinks just so I could sleep! I'll never do that again as long as I live!"

He did wear the rib belt. When we removed it three weeks later, the brave nurses in the room staggered out, swooning from the smelly vapors. They had a few choice words for Cy, none of which would have helped to get him into heaven.

At the end of office hours, before I started the paperwork, I sat smoking a cigarette in my consultation room. I thought about some of the things that endeared Cy to me and to the community. He operated a steak sandwich booth at the local fairs during the summer. He wore a white undershirt while he was attending the booth. As the T-shirts became soiled and sweat-laden, he hung them on a string above the counter where he prepared and sold the steak sandwiches. He did a very thriving business, despite the pungent aroma from the shirts, which cannot be described in polite English.

Cy fancied himself a ladies' man. Picture him at five feet six inches, weighing about 220 pounds, give or take ten, toothless, rarely shaven, and wearing a filthy cap. The cap could give a history of his whereabouts for the last thirty years. He spoke frequently about a cabin in the woods, his rendezvous place for his women. He bragged that he could make love to four or five women in a day, every day of the week. I had heard such tales from Marines, and I always doubted the credibility of the narrator. Cy was no exception.

One day, he came into my office in a rage and loudly demanded an answer from me. "What the hell did you do to Elsie B.? She had a perfect figger and you ruined her!"

"I just put her on a diet, Cy. She's diabetic, you know, and she was a hundred pounds overweight."

"Overweight, @?*&! She wasn't a pound overweight! She had a perfect figger and now she's just a (blankety-blank) stick! Damn you, Doc, you really messed her up."

It apparently did not matter to Cy that Elsie was married to *Mister* B. It seemed that she was part of his stable of women, either real or imaginary. If Elsie was representative of the women he took to his cabin, I can begin to understand his success with women. Knowing that he had trouble walking up one flight of stairs, I still had my doubts about his sexual prowess. He bragged even more outrageously in his youth than when I knew him. His contemporaries called him "Hubva Dollar Cy."

I asked my buddy, Lloyd Himmelberger, why Cy had that nickname and what it meant. He told me that about the time Cy was seventeen, he made a bet with someone that he could swallow a half dollar coin. Lloyd believed that the bet was for two dollars, but he wasn't certain. In any event, Cy swallowed a half dollar and won the bet. Since the half dollar was supplied by another person, Cy checked every day to see if the half dollar had successfully traveled his alimentary canal. When it did not appear after a week, he became worried and sought the help of a doctor.

The doctor happened to be Calvin Rentschler, MD, a Mayo-trained surgeon, and a character in his own right. X-rays showed that the coin was lodged in Cy's stomach. The coin failed to pass through the duodenum. Surgery was required to remove it. After the coin was removed surgically, Cy asked for the half dollar, as it was his property.

Cy neglected to pay Dr. Rentschler for the surgery. Dr. Rentschler finally asked him when he intended to pay the bill. Cy inquired if Dr. Rentschler had ever removed a fifty cent piece from a stomach before. Of course, he had not. Upon obtaining this admission, Cy informed the surgeon that since he was practicing surgery on his stomach, Cy did not owe anything for the surgery. He went on to say that he was not going to charge Dr. Rentschler any money for practicing on him.

I was finishing up the removal of a sebaceous cyst one busy afternoon when my receptionist came in to the surgical room.

"Doctor, there has been an accident on the Strausstown Road. Harold Cypress drove into a truck, and he is badly hurt."

I asked my senior nurse, Gloria, whom I trained as the first practicing physician's assistant in Pennsylvania, to finish up with the surgical patient. I ran to my car and sped to the Strausstown Road. Just above Way-Har, a dairy store owned by my patients Wayne and Harold Lesher, an access road came in at a sharp angle to Route 183. A tractor-trailer was turning into this road when Cy's little Volkswagen rammed into the front of the tractor-trailer.

Harold was unfortunately a drinking man. I never knew him to miss a day of heavy drinking. Arriving at the scene, I found him slumped over the wheel of his car, a large quantity of blood in his lap, and with no signs of life. He had a fatal chest injury with associated internal injuries. The state cops were there by that time. I could do nothing but to tell them that he was dead. After the family was notified, I drove back to the office. I was extremely distressed over his death. I was also very angry with him, surprised by my own voice.

"Cy!" I said out loud, "you stupid ass! You never even tried to stop drinking!"

Cy was a character, but under all of that tarnished *façade*, there was an inkling of his true self. Perhaps his alcoholism overrode any other aspect of his personality. Even though one could easily label him as a drunk, the reasons why he drank were never revealed to me. Surely one component had to be the need to "be somebody." Cy wanted to be recognized as a person who had achieved some status, even if that status was based on his ability to consume vast quantities of alcohol. He was loyal to his friends and helpful in every possible way to his neighbors. That he was notoriously unfaithful in his marriage was known by everyone, including Mrs. Cypress, who was a fine woman and quietly suffered his insults. His character was in many ways quite complex.

Back at the office, we picked up our hours and worked through the day, but my thoughts never for a moment left the tragedy of Harold Cypress. Alcoholism is a killer, and I knew it was just a matter of time until he killed himself or someone else in an accident. Cy's passing would certainly leave a vacuum in the Bernville community. With all his faults, he was known to be a generous and kind neighbor.

It is not easy to find a particular house or farm in the country when the roads are not marked with signs. This was the case when I first came to the Bernville area. Except for the streets in town, none of the country roads were marked. I would receive directions like this when a request for a housecall came in: "Go three miles toward Rehrersburg from Bernville, and turn right at the Zerbe farm. A mile and a half past the Zerbe farm, you'll see a large oak tree. That is the entrance to our lane, and we are the second farm on the right." Little did I know that Zerbe had been dead for a hundred years, and the farm was currently owned by someone named Miller. Fortunately, most of the names were painted on the mailboxes.

I was called by the Veterans Administration in the fall of 1964 to visit a Spanish American war veteran, Charles Ringler, aged ninety-six, who lived with a woman known locally as the *Hundzgranny,* or "dog's granny." Rosa Market was called the Hundzgranny because she had a habit of taking in stray dogs. She took care of at least thirty to forty dogs on her property. Charles Ringler was afflicted with pernicious anemia and needed periodic injections of vitamin B_{12}. The nurse who had been giving him the shots for years had moved away. They were looking for a replacement. This required a new doctor to see him and prescribe treatment. The road on which he lived had formerly been the road connecting Bernville to Strausstown, a torturous dirt road with hills and valleys and several sharp, hairpin turns. The caller described the house as not too far from the school, set up from the road, and accessible by a flight of wooden steps.

I started down the dirt and gravel road that veered sharply to the left, then up a small hill and down again, twisting and turning, and finally uphill again. There, perched on the side of a hill, was a dilapidated makeshift, two-room bungalow. There was no obvious parking area, so I pulled as close to the shoulder as possible. I took my bag from the car and approached the steps. Calling them steps was a stretch. What was before me was more like a Marine obstacle course in poor repair. The rickety, splintered railing did not promise much help. I made my way to what seemed to have been a porch at one time. Before I even raised my hand to knock on the door, a sickening odor of unidentifiable origin greeted me. Then a gravelly female voice croaked, "Come in."

The door opened and out gushed the foulness of hell. Every body sense was assailed with noxious stimuli: a cacophony of countless barking dogs, a stifling, suffocating, stercoraceous odor that gripped my nostrils, and an unbelievable scene before my eyes. About fifteen small dogs were tied to various objects, jumping and barking, animal feces and urine everywhere. In the midst of this chaos and filth was a disheveled elderly woman, screaming at the dogs and gesticulating to them in a threatening manner, trying to quiet the uncontrollable menagerie. Sitting on a small cot to my left was the patient.

The *hundzgranny* closed the door as I introduced myself. Turning to the patient, I explained I was here to give him his injection. I found a spot on the table that was not littered with food or debris, placed my bag there, and quickly prepared his injection before nausea overcame me. As soon as I withdrew the needle, I rushed out to the porch and vomited. Slightly recovered, I reentered the house and explained that I was allergic to dogs, which was not true. The screaming woman was relentless in her attempts to control those diabolical animals.

My patient, who appeared to be a congenial and vigorous man in his nineties, asked if I wanted to stay for a piece of pie. I barely had time to tell him I would be back in two weeks before I had to leave and throw up again. I was completely shaken. I decided that if that room was anything like hell, I would be a saint for the rest of my life. I did not know how I could ever go back there again or ask any of my nurses to go there. I could hardly wait to take a shower and change clothes. I was certain the odor of that place had permeated right through my clothes to my skin. How wonderful the crisp cold air felt surging through my lungs and washing out that foul air!

After a shower and a clean scrub suit, I sat with my staff to tell them about this horrifying experience. They could neither picture nor believe the scene I tried to describe. I said I would not ask for volunteers, but I wanted them to think of a way we could give the patient his needed injections without being subject to the horror of that room. One of the nurses suggested this was a perfect place for Cy, the irascible character in town for whom neither cleanliness nor Godliness was a major concern. He certainly would not mind filth or the odor. I hit upon the perfect plan, which required subterfuge to induce my patient to help me with the housecalls to the *hundzgranny's*. I told Cy I was allergic to dogs and could not go into the house. I would pay him to go with me to help our veteran out onto the porch, where I could give him his injection. He was very happy when I proposed it. We agreed on three dollars a trip. I was making only a dollar and a half from the VA for the injection, but it was well worth the additional time and money to avoid that room.

In time, I had one of the nurses accompany Cy to give the injections. I never saw the Spanish-American war veteran or the *hundzgranny* again. About two years later, Cy stopped by the office to tell me he'd found them both dead. With no small degree of entitlement, Cy told me that before he left the scene, he took the two smoked hams they had hanging in the back room.

While I was learning the cultural idiosyncrasies of the locals, I also cared for certain families who may have become isolated because of extreme poverty, mental illness, or some disability that kept them out of the mainstream.

I received a call from a neighbor to report that Woody Root was having "a fit." With a little questioning, I determined it was a grand mal seizure. It was late on a spring evening when I arrived at the house.

The cabin was located on the downside of a sloping hill without the luxury of steps. I was only able to locate the cabin from the smoke pouring from their chimney, which rose above the grassy hill. After crossing a field of high grass, I had to negotiate a steep, grassy slope in order to reach the cabin door. The home did not have electricity, running water, or plumbing.

Woody's convulsive seizure had terminated by itself. He was sitting on a kitchen chair, drooling. His brother Ralph sat next to him, and the older sister stood in the doorway between the kitchen and the bedroom. The father was out gathering wood for the stove. All of the occupants had limited mental capacity, but they were able to converse rationally and maintain an orderly but crowded home. Ralph was a very talented artist. He worked only in pencil and sketched mainly birds and other forms of wildlife. He had a keen eye for detail and a skillful hand. I am sure he could have sold his drawings, but he was not interested. I do not believe in the years that I knew him he spoke more than ten words. I learned from Woody that he'd had epilepsy since he was a child and was receiving medicine from the neurological clinic at the Reading Hospital. I checked his medication. Further questioning revealed he had missed both his evening and his morning doses, because he had misplaced the medicines. Upon examining him, I found that he had pharyngitis, a sore throat, with a slight fever, which I was able to treat with penicillin. When I suggested he come to the office in three days, he said they had no car and that they had to walk to Bernville to buy groceries. I had seen all three of them walking back and forth on Highway 183. Shirley and Woody were constantly talking and gesturing as they walked along, but Ralph seemed always to be quiet.

About a year later, while I was at the hospital making rounds, I was surprised by a call from Woody, who telephoned from a neighbor's. It seems Shirley "had it in her belly," which translated to abdominal pain. He could not explain further except to say that she had it all morning. I told him I could not get there for about one hour. He said that would be all right but urged me to come as soon as I could.

When I arrived at the house about an hour later, I found Shirley lying on the bed, her legs drawn up and spread. A newborn baby was on the bed, with the umbilical cord still attached and the placenta not yet expressed. They all looked at me and smiled, pointing to the baby. Woody never mentioned his sister was pregnant or in labor when I questioned him over the phone about the nature of her discomfort. They had a scissors, string, and rubbing alcohol waiting. Her father had delivered all three of his children. After tying off the cord and separating it from the newborn girl, I turned to Shirley to remove the placenta, happy that it had detached from the uterus and was lying in the vagina. We cleaned up the baby. Shirley dressed her and placed her in a laundry basket that served as a crib. A folded, torn quilt functioned as the mattress. I told Shirley I would see them again in a week. As I left the house walking through the kitchen, it occurred to me that the house now had electricity, and I noticed that they had acquired a television set, though there were no electric lights.

About a month later, I was called to testify in court. Shirley was suing the alleged father for support. Shirley was a tall, gangly woman, with straight, black, chaotic hair, not many teeth, and had had no chance to develop social graces. The alleged father was a merchant marine. The case hinged on the baby being full-term, which is defined as a birth weight of five and a half pounds. Most general practitioners do not carry baby scales when making a housecall. I did not weigh little Mary at the time of her birth. The accused father's lawyer made a huge issue of this, claiming that the baby was premature. Since his client had been at sea, he could not have been the father. I told the judge that this baby was a fat baby. Nature does not waste resources on fat in prematures. Of the several hundred babies I had delivered, I had never seen a fat preemie. In fact, that would be an oxymoron. The defense continued to badger me. I finally turned to the judge and said, "Your Honor, it is utterly impossible for this baby to have been premature. If this was the case, we would have to rewrite all the medical books and establish that Berks County has the largest premature ever born."

Though the judge did not laugh out loud, I saw him suppress a spreading smile. The jury was convinced that we had a fullterm baby. Shirley won the award, and paternity was established. I saw her daughter, Mary, only a few times over the next three years, mainly for acute childhood illnesses. When she went to school, I was notified by the courthouse that I had not filled out a birth certificate for her. I obtained a blank birth certificate from the hospital, and I noted the date and time. From Mary's chart kept in the office, I was able to fill out everything except her weight, which I estimated at eight and a half pounds.

Today's attitudes toward privacy are very different than they were during my practice. Even in the "let it all hang out" period of the late 60's, I uncovered dark, unspoken elements of human sexuality. Deviant behavior knew no class boundaries. I treated patients suffering from abuse in both backwoods cabins and landscaped ranch houses. A quote from Dr. William Osler inspired the title for the next chapter, chiding the young for succumbing to the base instincts of dominance, pride and the temporary pleasures of misguided passions.

"Who serve the gods die young. Venus, Bacchus, and Vulcan send in no bills in the seventh decade."

Dr. William Osler, Aphorism 187,
cited by William B. Bean, MD.

CHAPTER 10

Venus Renders Her Bill

The amount of sex education received by medical students in the United States is almost nil. The anatomy and physiology of sex is well explained if you happen to read the back of the textbook. I cannot recall a single lecture on human sexuality in the four years of medical school. It is still true today. In the first year of my practice, I came across some serious marital problems that were of a sexual nature. I was able to offer some help. When a sexual problem arises in marriage, it is most often very complex, not easily solved. I referred a fair number of these patients to a psychiatrist, who has had many years of experience with sexual matters. In most cases, couples come into marriage with enough sexual baggage to generate a host of problems. In others, infidelity is the issue. Sometimes ignorance, inconsideration, or outright stubbornness is the root of the problem. One thing is certain. Every sexual act has a consequence, both an immediate and a long-term effect. Sex is such a strong physiologic drive. I am always surprised that so many people view it as a trivial action. I encountered the devastating effect of infidelity on a marriage with a patient who came to see me with a physical complaint. Sometimes a general practitioner has to act as a psychologist when the body gives clues that all is not well in the topknot.

On a cold winter evening, a professional woman I had known for several years came into the office, complaining about severe abdominal pain. Forty-two years old, she was a popular and well-respected woman. I had seen her for acute bronchitis only once before this appointment. In my consultation room, she sat before me describing the pain and her other symptoms, mechanically pulling and shredding her handkerchief. She was sitting on the edge of the chair. When she finished describing her symptoms and signs, I looked at her and asked, "Claire, why don't you tell me your real problem?"

She startled and then burst into tears, burying her face in her handkerchief. She sobbed most uncontrollably. Her handkerchief was so mangled I gave her new tissues to dry her eyes and blow her nose. Then she started to talk.

"I am so ashamed, so humiliated, and so disgusted with myself that I don't know what to do. Please help me, Doctor. Just about a month ago, I went to a convention. I met a colleague there who was a very interesting man. We spent a lot of time together during the convention. One night, he asked me to go to dinner with him. After we had dinner and a few drinks, we went back to my hotel room to finish our conversation. One thing led to another, and before I knew it, we were in bed together. We had sex."

She burst into tears again. This time her whole body was shaking. I said nothing. She soon regained her composure. After a few minutes, she started speaking again.

"I was so upset I left the conference. I could not face that man again. I felt dirty and disgraced. I just wanted to run away and hide somewhere. I did not know how I could face my husband, Tim, again. My guilt is so great I can hardly bear it. I know if I tell Tim about what I did, it would totally destroy him! What can I do, Doctor, what can I do?"

This is an age-old problem. The conventional wisdom is "what you don't know can't hurt you," but in this case, it was slowly killing my patient. As a physician, my first duty was to save this woman's life. I explained to her that she had most likely created this stomach problem from her guilt. We would need first to determine whether she actually had an ulcer. Her symptoms suggested that she did. After we had made an assessment of her physical condition and started treatment, we would tackle the more difficult problem of handling her guilt by trying to resolve the conflict. A conversion reaction of this nature can be severe enough to cause a perforated ulcer. She was a woman with a very strong conscience, who had made a serious mistake, and was paying a terrible price.

Her x-rays showed a gastric ulcer that was of considerable size but not yet perforated. I placed her on anti-anxiety medication and additional medication to help control her gastric secretion. I prescribed some dietary restrictions, particularly caffeine and alcohol, along with a host of other recommended foods. Her physical symptoms improved, but her anxiety remained.

The following month, we met again to discuss whether or not she would tell her husband about the affair. She deeply loved Tim, which intensified her guilt. Tim was a good man and a good husband. He was about five foot eight inches with a slight build, wavy black hair, and a serious look on his face most of the time. Tim was a white-collar worker with a responsible position. They had been married more than twenty years, and it seemed to be a happy marriage. As in many of the marriages I have known, his wife was a major source of strength and support for Tim. My gut feeling was that her confession would be a devastating blow to him. On the other hand, if she continued to feel the degree of guilt she was now experiencing, it would only escalate and could do her irreparable harm.

As we sat in my consultation room, Claire had the appearance of a beaten and dejected animal. She did not want to hurt her husband Tim, and she wanted to save her marriage. The situation was like an accidental discharge of a firearm which kills a loved one. There was no intention to harm, but the result was irreversible. The one thing I thought she could count on was that the love her husband had for her would be enough to sustain him through the devastation of knowing she had been unfaithful. Claire said she was not capable of doing this alone. She asked if she could bring her husband in for a conference with the three of us. She felt she would be able to tell him then. I agreed to this arrangement. We made an appointment on an evening that I did not have office hours so that we would not be disturbed. I turned off the office phone and explained to Joanne that she would get all the calls at "the clinic phone", an extension I had previously installed at our home.

I arranged chairs so that the three of us would be sitting together, placing her beside her husband. After we sat down, I explained to Tim the nature of Claire's illness. I told him she had a gastric ulcer which was induced by stress. Only by relieving the cause of the stress would she be able to return to good health. He was very cooperative and agreed we should do whatever we had to do to help her to get better. Tim took her hand, as if to reassure her of his support and belief she would get better. Claire told Tim that her stress was due to guilt. She was guilty because she had been unfaithful to him at the time of the convention. She began to cry.

Tim was incredulous. If I had hit him with a club, he would not have been more surprised. He was not sure what he had heard and asked her to repeat it. In a halted manner, with much sobbing, she related the episode again. She begged his forgiveness over and over. When Tim finally realized what she had said, he was a crushed man. The blood had drained from his face. He was not angry, but terribly, terribly hurt. At this point, I started to talk.

"Tim, your wife loves you very much, so much that she was willing to die rather than to hurt you. She did not want you to know about this incident, because she knew you would be hurt. Unless she can resolve the guilt, there is no way that she can be treated. She would eventually die from a bleeding ulcer. I told her, because of the love that you have for each other, it was essential that you knew about this incident in order for her to heal. I know you find it difficult to believe that this happened, but it did. You must understand that if she had any positive feeling about this other man, she would not have had an ulcer. It is impossible for her to live with this guilt because of her feeling for you."

I paused, trying to observe Tim's response. He reminded me of shell-shocked soldiers. His world had collapsed. His loving, faithful wife no longer existed. He felt betrayed, used, a nothing. It was the first time I ever witnessed anyone in a state of despair, beyond depressed. Any additional explanation would not have reached him. Tim's sorrow was implacable. He had crawled into a deep dark hole, shutting out the reality of what he heard. I could see his pain and feel his desperation. His facial expressions telegraphed the intensity of his despair to me. Had he been any less of a man, he would have become enraged and potentially violent. It is natural to destroy whatever is hurting you or trying to hurt you. In Tim's case, the love for his wife drove him to this point of devastation. I was not witnessing jealousy. This was love betrayed.

In that instant, Tim also became my patient. I needed to do what I could for his survival medically, as he faced the emotional devastation of his shattered heart and his now tenuous marriage. I decided an antidepressant was an appropriate tool for Tim.

An assessment of suicidal potential is not an infallible process. There are certain obvious signs, but the physician can never be certain about what is in his patient's mind. In Tim's case, having known him for several years and knowing that he was a stable, responsible person, I believed that he was not suicidal. I had seen antidepressant medication work minor miracles on some patients. The more severe the depression, the less effective they were, but in a way, because of the pharmacological process they evoke, they are capable of acting as a buffer against self-destruction. With Tim, I believed that at this time he needed that extra bit of help. Over the next month or so, he would walk not only in the Valley of the Shadow, but tread the pathway of his own personal hell.

I made an appointment to see him in a week, hoping that he would keep the appointment. I did not feel that he was suicidal, but it is impossible to tell with some patients. The last thing I said to him was, "Tim, only God knows how you feel. I know you believe in God and attend church regularly. Share this burden with God and pray that he gives you understanding and strength. Between our visits, feel free to call me anytime, for any reason, if you need help."

They left the office. I have never seen two more dejected and unhappy people. I prayed that God would give them both the strength to see this through. The next two to three days would be unbearable for both of them. Tim would have many sleepless nights ahead and some terrible days. The weekends would be even more terrible. Their sexual life would be over for a while, but I felt it would be part of the pathway back to their loving relationship.

The months passed. I saw Tim every month, and we spent hours together as he poured out his heart to me. He was filled with sorrow, anger, and despair, a scarred soul laid bare.

On a snowy winter night about three months into his depression, Tim appeared in the office for his regular monthly visit. He had the hound dog facial expression, typical of many depressed patients. His handshake was almost cadaverous. I asked him how he was doing and how he felt.

His reply spoke volumes.

"I am alive, Doctor, but that's about all. There seems to be no reason, no purpose, no direction to my life now. I have lost faith in just about everything. Even my faith in God is tenuous. I don't see the world as bright and shiny, a place of happy smiling faces any more. I see a gray-black dismal world, where everyone lies, cheats, and cannot be trusted. My nights are horrible periods of darkness. My mornings are only slightly better. For me, it is always a gray, rainy day. I am distant from the one person I love. The abyss separating us seems endless."

"Does the medication help?" I asked.

"I don't know, Doctor, I take it. It must be helping, because I'm still alive."

"You mean you're thinking of suicide, Tim?"

"I have thought of it, but it is against all my beliefs. Sometimes I see this depression as a cross I must carry, but I do not know how long I can bear it."

"Tim, I believe the hell you are going through will not last much longer," I told him. "From what you are saying, I can see the beginnings of a resolution. No one knows better than you that you have a way to go. Remember the love you have for Claire. The love she has for you has not diminished. It is still very much alive, and believe it or not, it is growing." I tried to reassure him.

"I hope so, Doctor," he replied quietly.

As he left the office, I noticed the way he was carrying his body. His step seemed slightly lighter. I felt he was on the way to recovery. I said a short prayer, thanking God for His helping hand.

Two months later, Claire came into the office with Tim. They appeared to be moving closer toward each other, even sharing a hopeful smile as they sat down across from me. I continued to see them, separately and together. Each month, there was a little more light, and Claire's stomach problems were lessening. One evening, Tim told me that he had turned a corner in his thinking and shared with me a revelation.

"Doctor, for the first time in my life, I have a vision of God as an all-merciful being. Though I studied a little philosophy in college, I never really understood the nature of God, until I reached this point of desperation. God forgives us again and again when we turn our backs on him, reject him, after he has given his very life for us. To be able to forgive like that must indeed be a divine quality."

Tim had discovered one of the most profound teachings of theology. It was a breakthrough. While searching for God in his quest for help, Tim had connected with the merciful nature of God. It was a very short distance between that understanding and his ability and will to forgive his wife. I recalled some of the profound associations between pain and forgiveness described by some great theologians. Tim had expressed the severe pain he was feeling from his wife's betrayal, and I needed to address that.

"Tim, the past is the source of your pain," I said to him. "It has a tyrannical grip on you. The only way you can free yourself from the pain is to free yourself from the past, and this you can do only by forgiveness." Tim was listening intently.

"The desire for payback can distort and corrupt our true feelings. It is a costly experience to forgive and costly to be forgiven, for a real wrong. Forgiveness is a true expression of love, and it is near as Godlike as we can ever become. I know you understand what I am saying."

I watched carefully to see his expression, for I knew this was a pivotal moment. Either he would forgive Claire, or he would sink into a deeper depression. His face, initially emotionless, slowly formed into a smile, the first in many months. His next words were, "I understand, Doctor. The healing is now up to me."

It was an extraordinary breakthrough. Tim was searching for God. He was looking for help and found the merciful nature of God. I don't know if the antidepressants were of any value, but shortly after this, he asked me if he could stop this medication. I said we would cut it down first and then stop it altogether. His leave-taking handshake was a firm grip for the first time. I knew it would take time for them to be back in a loving relationship. Though there were scars, their love would be stronger than before this incident. Claire was with him on the next visit. They were a restored, healing, mature couple.

One early Sunday morning about 1:30, my phone rang. The voice on the other end was one I recognized, but it was overlaid with great anxiety. The caller wanted to meet me at the office, stating that he had a personal problem he could not discuss over the phone. I asked him if he could wait until morning. He insisted on seeing me as soon as possible, because it was a true medical emergency. Since I did not know him to be a man who was easily excitable, I told him I would meet him at my office in twenty minutes. When I arrived, he was waiting in his car in the parking lot. I greeted him, unlocked the office, and we went up to the treatment rooms. As he walked, he kept his hand over his crotch. He was hobbling with some difficulty.

Once in the treatment room, he removed his trousers, without saying a word to me. He revealed a bloody pair of shorts. I had him lie down on the examining table and helped him to remove his shorts in order for me to see the nature of his problem. Though there was no profuse bleeding, his penis and testicles were covered with wet clotted blood. I asked him what had happened. Had he been in an accident? He was embarrassed as he explained the nature of his injury. He had a small cabin on Summer Mountain Road where he had taken a girlfriend earlier that evening. The sparsely furnished cabin had a regulation military cot on which they were having sex. Military cots are designed for a single occupant, generally not over 250 pounds. The suspension spring system consists of steel slats and small open-ended springs that serve as the only mattress support. In the throes of passion, he misjudged the mechanics of the operation and rammed his penis into one of the holding springs on the side of the bed. A large, ragged two-inch tear resulted. When I saw him, a clot had formed in the semi-erect penis. The bleeding had been reduced to a small oozing. I had never repaired any injury like this. I told him he should go to the hospital and have it done by a urologist. He pleaded with me to repair it because his wife would find out and his marriage would be over if he went to the hospital.

As much as I disliked doing it, I called an old-time friend and colleague for his advice. I apologized for waking him at such a dreadful hour and explained the situation. He told me exactly how to make the repair. He advised me to make sure I inserted a catheter first to avoid the danger of sewing the urethra shut. As long as I could see a steady flow of urine, everything would be okay. I thanked him profusely and then set about the task of repairing this awful laceration. First, I blocked the nerves at the base of the penis. This resulted in pain relief and caused the penis to return close to normal size with some extrusion of the clots. I could remove the remaining clots easily, as I inserted the catheter. The deep tissues were repaired with very fine absorbable suture material. I noticed that only the superficial artery and vein were injured and the deep artery was undamaged. The skin and Colles' fascia were closed with the same type suture material. This would not leave a visible scar or any signs of a recent wound.

When he expressed extreme gratitude, I explained to him that he was not out of the woods completely, because we were not sure how this injury would heal. With luck, there would be minimal scarring and no urinary tract complications. Before he left, I removed the catheter. We sat and smoked a cigarette while I tried to explain to him without preaching that the consequences of infidelity are sometimes far-reaching. He had a wonderful wife, and he was damn lucky to have her. He said he had learned from this and that it was not likely he would stray again. I told him I wanted to see him in a week and asked him to give me a call if he had any problems in the meantime.

He made a full recovery with a modest amount of scarring that caused a slight deviation to the right of his penis with a full erection. I explained that with time it might correct itself. He said he could live with this. I don't know if he continued his Summer Mountain adventures. We never discussed it again. Last I knew, he was still married and his children were both in college.

One evening during office hours, a teenage girl appeared complaining of having "two spiders in my eye." When my nurse, Pearl, ushered her into the treatment room, she whispered that this girl was not the sharpest knife in the drawer. She was about eighteen, attractive, smartly dressed, and looked worried. To my knowledge, there are no reports of a spider ever being in anybody's eye, though I'm sure this must have happened at some time in the history of mankind. The most obvious cause would be a crab louse. Using a small magnifying lens, I picked one of these ugly parasites from her eyebrow and placed it on a microscope slide. Examination showed that it was a *Pediculosis pubis,* or common crab louse.

"What does it look like?" she asked as I was examining the specimen.

"Here, take a look," I said as I got up from the chair and offered her the microscope.

She sat down, took one look at the still alive crab louse, turned to me with her eyes widely open, and said, "Was that on my eye?!"

"That's it."

She fainted, almost hitting the floor before I was able to grab her by her shoulders. Pearl and I lifted her on the treatment table and removed her clothes. She was heavily infested with crab lice. While she was unaware and in no danger, we treated her with Quell cream. When she awoke, she was shaking, but aware of her situation.

"How did I get this?" she wanted to know.

"Do you have a boyfriend in the Marine Corps or the military?" I asked.

"Yes, I am dating a Marine," she said.

"Was he home recently?"

"Yes, about two months ago."

"That is where you got them." I explained that many of the Marines are infested with crab lice and that they are treated periodically. I did not explain that crab lice are generally a consequence of promiscuous sexual activity. Instead, I explained that they are transmitted from person-to-person and left the rest up to her. She seemed upset. When I saw her a week later, now free of her infestation, she was wiser, leading to me to believe she would be not quite as sexually free the next time.

One afternoon during regular office hours, a young girl of about seventeen called for an appointment complaining of "severe pain down there." We gave her a late afternoon appointment. When she appeared, she was obviously in a great deal of pain. Examination of her pelvic area showed an extensive viral infection with *herpes genitalis* in an acute phase. She had recently graduated from high school and obtained a job in a local clothing factory. There she met a man who had pressured her for sexual activity. She resisted for about two months but finally consented. She had had intercourse two weeks before she noticed the sores on her vaginal surface. She said they spread and became very painful in a few days, so painful that she could not ride her bicycle to work. The appearance of lesions and the distribution suggested *herpes genitalis* type II.

I explained to her that the lesions would most likely subside within two weeks. She needed to be aware that they could recur as often as three or four times a year for the first year, but that they could eventually stop.

She looked at me with a very innocent expression and made it plain that she had not wanted to have sex with the man. He had pressed her, and she gave in only once. She said she would never do it again. I saw her twice over four weeks. During one of the visits, she told me that she had discovered that the man she had been dating was married and had two children. She was horrified and felt so ashamed. She said she did not understand why people wanted to do this, with all the trouble it makes. She did not get anything out of it except pain and a doctor's bill.

I comforted her and told her that she had learned something. Relations with people have consequences. She should know much more about a person before she entered into an intimate relationship. That was her take-home lesson. She should know that there were good men in the world, who would not pressure her for sex. That was always a sign that they were worth marrying.

I saw her only once again, about four years later, when she came in with her fiancé for required serology tests prior to marriage. She had been dating this young man for more than a year. I prayed that the lessons of her past would help her in choosing a life partner who would honor and protect her, and truly love her. A card arrived on my desk to let me know they had moved to Indiana, after they were married.

CHAPTER 11

Sins of the Father

Shortly after arriving in Bernville and starting my practice, I came up against several cases of incest. These involved mainly fathers and daughters, with two cases of grandfathers and granddaughters. My first case was a fifteen-year-old girl who presented with headaches and abdominal pain. She was a tall, large-boned girl, with straight mousey hair. Her skin was pale, and her blue eyes had a sadness about them. She sat quietly on the examining table, her head bent forward, her eyes fixed on her knees while she slowly swung her feet back and forth. She'd had these symptoms on and off for several years. Now they were causing her to miss a considerable amount of school. Her mother had made the appointment but was unable to give me very much history. When I spoke to the girl, she was not very communicative. Her mother answered most of the questions and made the only comments. At the time I examined the girl, I did not do a pelvic exam, centering my interest mainly on her abdomen. Since I could not demonstrate any abnormality of the abdominal cavity by palpation, I suggested a flat plate of the abdomen.

After scheduling the x-ray, I discussed her dietary habits and made a few suggestions. She had neither vomiting nor constipation, nothing to suggest a major gastrointestinal disease. The next morning, I checked with the school to see how she was doing academically. The principal was very cooperative and told me that she was an above-average student but that her grades were beginning to fall markedly in the last six months. I thanked him and let him know that she was being considered for hospital evaluation.

The flat plate x-ray was negative as I expected. I began to believe this girl had a psychosomatic illness. A few days later, the pain became increasingly worse. I suggested we hospitalize her for further investigation. Her father was not happy about this, but her mother agreed to have her hospitalized. She entered the hospital that evening. After office hours, I drove to the hospital to complete her admission workup. It was the first time that I had an opportunity to speak with her alone. When I asked her to tell me more about her abdominal pain, she broke into tears. Sitting on the edge of the bed, she rocked back and forth.

"I don't know how to tell you this," she said, "but my father is at me all the time."

When I asked her what she meant by "at her all the time," she replied, "He wants to have sex with me all the time!"

Shocked, I asked her how long this had been going on. "

Since I was ten," she sobbed.

"Can you tell me more about it, how it happened?" I asked. "Does your mother know about it?"

She gathered herself together, determining what to tell me and what to omit. She looked so helpless and alone. As she began to talk, relief came over her face. She was obviously frightened about what she was telling me. She spoke very softly, almost inaudibly, but as she spoke, the tempo increased and so did the volume.

"When I was growing up, my mother had radiation treatment for cancer. She could no longer sleep with my father. One night, my mother took me out of bed and brought me over to my father's bed. She said my father needed a woman, and she was not able to take care of him anymore. I would have to take her place. I did not understand what she was talking about. She left me with my father and went to sleep in my bed. My father told me to get in bed with him, and he began to feel me all over. He started to kiss me. I pushed him away. He grabbed me and told me that I would do whatever he wanted me to do or I would be really sorry. He made me hold his thing, while he felt me between my legs. He showed me how to move it up and down.

"I was scared and crying all the time. He said that I would get used to it, and I would like it. This went on every night for about two weeks, and then he tried to put his thing in me. It hurt so much I hollered and hollered. He stopped that night, but he kept trying again every night. One night while he tried, I started to bleed. I was scared and ran out of the room to my mother. I told her what happened, and she said it would be all right, it would stop in a little while. I spent the night with her and pleaded with her not to send me back in there with him. She said that if I would not do it, he would probably kill both of us. I could not stand it any longer, everything about it made me ill. I hated to have him touch me, but I could not fight him off. I cried just about every night, I could not sleep. I was happy to be at school and away from home. I dreaded coming home. I spent as long a time on my lessons as I could, just to keep from going to bed. It made me sick just to think about him. Even the smell of him made me sick."

As I listened, I was filled with outrage. Her father had a position of prominence in the community and was well-respected.

Little did the town know what a monster he was. My initial impulse was to notify the authorities and have him arrested. My next thought was to get the girl out of the house to somewhere safe. I pictured her trying to fight off this brute of a man and being terrorized, not knowing what was going to happen to her.

I called her mother the next day and told her I wanted to see her that morning before I went to the hospital. I met her in my office. When I confronted her with what her daughter told me, she did not deny anything. She explained that she had cervical cancer with extensive radiation that scarred her vagina and made it impossible for her to have intercourse. Her husband threatened to leave them unless he could have sex. It was he who suggested that she substitute their daughter. She admitted she was horrified at the thought. Yet, she was no longer able to work and had three small children to support. She did not know what to do to keep her family together. She could not explain this to her young daughter, so she just took her over to him.

I explained that the law required that I report her husband as a sex offender. Most likely she would have to testify against him, and he would go to jail. She pleaded with me not to do this, because it would be devastating to her family. I told her that her daughter could not go back into her home. I would have her placed in a foster home until we could find a permanent place for her. She told me her own mother, who lived in the Midwest, would be happy to have her daughter. I felt that would be far enough to keep her father from bothering her. I warned that if he molested the other children in any way, I would notify the police without hesitation. She was distraught and fearful but agreed to call her mother to make arrangements to move her daughter there.

Later that day, I spoke with my young patient in the hospital. I explained what her mother and I had discussed and revealed that we were making arrangements for her to live with her grandmother. She was extremely happy.

She told me that she had dated a boy her own age, since she was in high school. Her father had beaten her because of this. He threatened that if she ever dated another boy he would give her a beating she would never forget. After this threat, the abdominal pain and the headaches became worse, and her grades started to fail.

Her mother did not have the money for train fare for a ticket out West. I bought the ticket and gave her some spending money. In exchange for my help, I told her mother that I wanted to see her husband. If he did not see me, I would send the constable around to get him. I was confident enough of his arrogance to know he would not risk shattering the public *façade* he'd created in his role as head of an influential community organization.

He made an appointment a few days later. He looked like an overgrown bully. When he came in, I told him that if he ever molested another of his children, I would bring the full weight of the law down on him. I explained that I believed the children should be separated from him, but I unwillingly went along with this arrangement because of his wife. Any hint of abuse of the other children, and I would have both children removed from the home and both parents prosecuted. He was sullen, but he knew I meant what I said.

We monitored the children carefully with periodic home visits by the school nurse. Three years later, the family moved away, and I never heard from the couple again. The daughter wrote to me to say she was doing very well in high school and had planned to go to nursing school. I wrote back that I was pleased that she was doing well and wished her every success. I did not hear from her again until she sent me an invitation to her graduation from nursing school.

###

There are some people born without a conscience. They believe that whatever they feel is good for them is a good thing. Anything that has a negative effect on them is bad. Lying, stealing, cheating, promiscuity, adultery, mayhem, or murders are not significant. All that matters is getting what they want. I came across a man like that one evening when he brought his two-year-old daughter to see me with a festering, ugly wound on her forehead. It had been neglected for some time. It would leave a very disfiguring scar, for it had eroded down to the dermis, the deep support structure beneath the skin. He had rigged up a protective cage and placed it over her head so that she would not scratch the wound or bang against an object. I asked him why he waited so long to bring his child in for treatment. He answered in an angry, arrogant way, "You doctors are just a bunch of money-hungry bastards! I can treat wounds better than you can."

He was a burly, angry-looking, unshaven man, who stood in a defiant position. He was constantly wetting his lips with his tongue, a snake-like gesture.

I ignored his remark and had the nurses place the little girl on the treatment table. She was a pretty little thing. Though in pain, she was sweet. After we removed the head apparatus, we carefully cleansed and debrided the wound. We applied antibiotic ointment, sterile dressings, and bandages. I told him to leave the wound closed. I would see the child again in three days. It was very important for him not to miss the appointment.

Three days later, the mother brought the child. Examination of the wound showed satisfactory progress. The infection had largely subsided and granulation tissue was moving in from the bottom, a part of the healing process. We dressed the wound again.

I spoke with the mother who looked like a badly neglected individual. She explained that she just had another child a year ago, who had been born at home. When I asked if she had a pelvic examination since the child was born, she said she had never had a pelvic examination. I offered to do an examination while she was at the office. She refused, explaining that her husband would never pay for it, because he did not approve of her going to a doctor. I told her I would not charge for it. I believed she should have a pelvic and a Pap smear. She agreed, and we did the examination and the test.

She had an eroded cervix which suggested a potential problem. The Pap smear report found a cervical carcinoma *in situ*. I called her and told her that she needed to go to the hospital to have treatment. She called me back and told me her husband would not permit her to go for treatment. I asked her to put him on the phone. He would not speak to me. I sent him a registered letter, informing him that his wife needed treatment. If she did not get treatment, she would develop cervical cancer and die. If he would not permit her to go for treatment, I would ask for a court order. I would not stand by and let his wife die. Under duress, he agreed, and she had the treatment and survived.

A more horrifying incident of ignorant depravity and abuse plagued the lives of this innocent mother and her children. This terrible man was a second husband to Virginia, as I will call her. Virginia had been widowed with three children from her first marriage, two boys and a girl, before her second marriage produced the two younger children. Her little girl, about twelve years old, sold strawberries from a small bridge on Route 183. She was a pleasant girl, always smiling and happy. Her stepfather, a welder by trade, came in and wanted to borrow a book on obstetrics. I asked him why he needed an obstetrical text book. He said he was just interested in obstetrics. I refused to let him borrow one. I told him if he wanted to learn about obstetrics and pregnancy he should go to the library. He left in a huff with his usual string of expletives.

A few months later, Virginia came into the office with the little strawberry girl, who was obviously pregnant and near full term. She told me that her husband was the father of the child and that he wanted to deliver the child. Horrified and outraged, I told Virginia that her daughter needed to be seen at the obstetrical clinic at the hospital. It is no easy matter to deliver a twelve-year-old child. I explained to her that social services would have to be contacted and that there were legal implications for her husband's role in fathering this child. She understood all of this. Though she would not press charges, she did want the best treatment for her daughter.

The young girl went to the obstetrics clinic and had the baby. She then went to live with her mother's sister in another state. I do not know if the baby was given out for adoption or raised by the aunt. I do know that the father did not go to jail. Two years later, he had a paralyzing stroke. He was able to walk only with difficulty and had lost most of his speech. He still continued to swear constantly, but he neither understood what was being said, nor was he able to respond intelligently. He died about six months later. Virginia and her family survived on his insurance and Social Security until the older children went to work. All of their lives improved considerably after the death of her second husband, one of the most difficult and amoral individuals I have ever met.

On a cold winter's night, we were about halfway through our scheduled patients when a distraught mother appeared with an eleven-year-old girl. The nurses put her into the gynecology examining room. When I saw her, she was wearing an examination gown. A note on the chart describing her reason for being there was cryptic. It read "statutory rape." Puzzled, I asked the mother, Arlene, why she had made the appointment for her daughter. She explained, stammering, that her daughter, Cindy, had been having sex with her older cousin, who worked for them as a farmhand. The mother had discovered the girl in bed with her eighteen-year-old male cousin two nights before. The girl denied having sex with him, saying she ran to his bed because she had a bad dream and was frightened. The mother explained that the girl's room adjoined the cousin's room and was next to the parents' bedroom. The room layout, in which it was necessary to go through one room to get into a second room, was typical of many a farmhouse I had seen. The girl's room had two doors, one to the parents' room and one to the cousin's room.

The mother wanted me to examine the girl to determine if she had had sexual intercourse. If so, she was going to have her nephew arrested for raping her daughter. The girl did not seem upset about having this examination. She sat quietly on the table, gently nibbling on her lower lip while twisting her long brown hair around her index finger. I asked the mother if she would mind leaving the room while I examined her daughter so that I could speak with the girl privately. She agreed. As the nurse was arranging Cindy on the examining table, I asked her if she had had sex with her cousin. She looked at me as though I was an idiot. "Yes, lots of times," she answered matter-of-factly.

"How long has this been going on?" I asked.

"Since Christmas last year," she shot back.

"And you never told your mother about this?"

"No, why should I?"

I didn't answer her. I told her I was going to examine her. She seemed to be tall for her age, medium-boned, clear skin, but her teeth were not in good condition. There were no signs of puberty, no breast bud, no axillary hair, no pubic hair, and no acne. Pearl had positioned her in stirrups and put out the vaginal speculum that we used on very young girls. I explained to Cindy what I was about to do. I found only small, tag-like remnants of a hymen. While performing a digital examination, I noticed the degree of relaxation of her vaginal muscles was marked. I had to use an adult speculum. When I examined the tissues of the vaginal walls, they appeared to be polished. There were no *rugae*, the ridges normally seen with vaginal tissue. Her vaginal surface suggested the inside of a polished cylinder. Her immature vaginal epithelium had struggled to provide protection from the many insults it suffered. Since she was not yet producing adequate estrogen, the lining of her vagina was fighting a losing battle. The rest of her examination was within normal limits.

As Cindy was getting dressed, I told Arlene that this young girl had been having regular intercourse, for a long period of time. She had not started her menstrual cycle, which would not occur before a year or more. Though she had consented to having sex with her cousin, this was a case of statutory rape, because of her age. I offered to testify if the mother wanted to prosecute the boy. Cindy had suffered a great injustice. Her childhood had gone, obliterated by the passions of a teenage boy, her innocence consumed by the selfish desires of an inconsiderate lout. The soft, gentle little girl had been transformed to a hardened, premature teenager. She assumed that having sex made her an adult. Now she knew it all. Cindy brought to mind the image of a beautiful flower crushed underfoot by the hobnail boots of a vandal.

Months later, the jury found Arlene's nephew guilty of statutory rape. If I remember correctly, his sentence was from two to five years in prison. The little girl was terribly upset. She threatened to kill herself but lived on to be an adult. I never saw her after the trial nor heard from the family again.

###

Of all reported cases of incest in the United States, around ten to fifteen percent involve siblings. There were several cases in my practice during a twenty-year period, each presenting in a different manner. The case I recall most clearly ended in near tragedy. I was called to a farm on a summer afternoon to see a teenage boy named Ron who had attempted suicide by cutting his wrists. I arrived at the farm and was surprised by the state of disorder of the equipment and vehicles and general disrepair of the buildings. The condition of the place was a red flag. The home was a wreck. Dirty clothes and dishes and trash and food containers were thrown everywhere. Sitting on a filthy sofa in the living room was a young man of eighteen or nineteen. He had a white cloth wrapped around each wrist. Ron's face was a picture of despair and desperation, mingled with anger. His father and mother were sitting on either side trying to comfort him. The father stood up to greet me. I had passed this farm many times, but I had seen this boy only once several years ago when he was very ill with pneumonia.

I examined his wrists to determine the severity of the lacerations. They were classic hesitation cuts, seen often in suicide attempts designed to get attention rather than to terminate life. I redressed the wound with sterile gauze and bandages. Pulling up a kitchen chair, I attempted to talk to the boy. Ron was not willing to talk about why he tried to kill himself. He became even more sullen and withdrawn.

I asked his father if he knew why Ron was depressed. He blurted out, "He loves his sister and is mad because she is dating another boy."

"Shut up!" Ron said to his father.

"Now, sonny, don't talk so mean to your father!" came from the mother. She was a care-worn, overworked, distraught wisp of a woman.

"Can you tell me about this?" I asked Ron.

"It's none of your damn business!" was his angry reply.

The mother stayed with the boy while I motioned the father to come into the kitchen with me. I explained to him that Ron was depressed and was a danger to himself and others. I recommended that he be hospitalized.

His father objected. Ron was needed to help with the milking. His father could not do it by himself. Ron going to the hospital would create a hardship on him and his wife. They could not afford any extra paid help.

I could do no more for Ron. I left the father with instructions to call me if anything happened in the next few days. I told him to bring Ron to the office in three days so that I could change the dressings. I thought better of giving him medication. Either he would not take what I prescribed, or he might take it all at once.

I had an uneasy feeling that this was not going to turn out well. This boy was a disaster waiting to happen. He was seething with anger and hatred, a pressure cooker waiting to explode. Ron was muscular and obviously very strong, surely a danger to his family, his sister, and her boyfriend. At ten o'clock that evening, a frantic call came into the office from Ron's father. Ron had taken a rifle and was looking for his sister and her boyfriend. I told the father and mother to stay put. I would call the state police. They did not know where their daughter was but assumed she was with her boyfriend. They believed he was from Hamburg but weren't sure where he lived. I described the farm to the state police and told them they could get a description of the car and the boy from his parents. I emphasized that Ron was potentially dangerous and urged extreme caution when they found him.

He would either end up in jail that evening or the state mental hospital. One way or the other, he had to be removed from his home and from society. An hour later, the state police called to let me know that they found Ron on the Shartlesville Road in a ditch. He had tried to negotiate a curve and ran off the road. They had handcuffed him and were taking him to the office so that I could commit him to the State Hospital. I made the arrangements and signed the necessary papers. They admitted him to a tight security facility at the hospital.

Before I went to the hospital the next morning to make rounds, I received a call from Ron's father. When they returned from the hospital the evening before, their daughter, Tess, had returned home. She was appalled and frightened by what had happened to her brother. She wanted to meet with me to see if she could help in any way. I suggested we meet in the office, because no one was in yet. We would have privacy. Within ten minutes, her car pulled into the driveway. She was a very attractive, seventeen-year-old girl. She was a true blonde with blue eyes. Tess appeared somewhat timid. I remembered treating her when she was eight for a laceration on her arm that occurred while climbing over a barbed wire fence. We sat facing each other in my consultation room. I needed to ask her a lot of questions about her relationship with her brother. She seemed to want to help, so I trusted she would tell the truth.

"Is it true that Ron is in love with you?" I asked outright.

"Yes," she answered with her head down, "we have been lovers since I was thirteen years old."

"Can you tell me about this? How did it happen?"

She stared at her lap as if trying to collect her thoughts. She took a deep breath, lifted her eyes to me, and said, "I have never spoken to anyone about my relationship with Ron. I am so worried about him now that I will tell you everything I know if it will help him to get better."

I assured her that except for the psychiatrist who would be treating him, I would put nothing on paper for anyone else to see.

"I was thirteen and Ron was fourteen and a half. We used to play together all the time after we were done with our chores. We had to help with the milking and feeding the cows twice a day. After we were finished, we would play around in the cow barn in the feed entry. He would chase me up to the hay loft, and we would wrestle on the hay. We had been doing that since I was nine. We had a lot of laughs and fun. One evening, when we were wrestling in the hay, he kissed me and held me very tightly. He looked me square in the face and kissed me again. He was very strong. I didn't know what to make of it. I broke loose and ran down the ladder and into the house.

"I was developing and had just gotten my period few months before. I did not want to wrestle with him anymore. A few days later, after we finished the milking and our parents had gone back to the house, we were cleaning up and putting things away. He came over to me from behind and grabbed my breasts. He took me by the arms, twisted me around and kissed me. His hands started to move all over me. I struggled to get away from him, but he was too strong for me. He told me he loved me and wanted to be with me forever. I was really scared. At the same time, I was thrilled that he loved me, because I always had strong feelings for him but never quite understood what I felt.

"He would spend a lot of time looking at me when we were alone together, just staring at me. I would try to say something to him, but I never knew what to say. One night after the milking, my parents left us to visit our grandma. We were alone in the house. I was doing my homework when he asked me to come upstairs. He wanted to show me something. I followed him into his bedroom. He put his arms around me and slowly put me down on his bed. He pulled up my dress and put his hand on me. He started to kiss me in a way that he had never done before.

"I was really frightened and tried to get up. He pleaded with me to be quiet, that he would not hurt me, and that he wanted me. I stopped fighting him. He pulled off my panties and took off his pants and got on top of me. The next thing, he was trying to put his penis in me. I kept telling him to stop, but he wouldn't stop. When he finished with me, he got up and cried and said he was so sorry, but he just loved me so much he had to do that. I don't know why, but I really felt sorry for him. He asked me not to tell our parents, and I said I would not say anything. That's how it got started."

She looked at me as a penitent would look at a confessor. She seemed to be relieved that she had unburdened her soul. She was still a very young girl who had been through a lot of emotional upheaval. She seemed mature beyond her years. She was extremely upset.

I tried to be as understanding as I could be to continue questioning her.

"How do you feel about your relationship now?"

She shifted in her seat, swallowed nervously, and replied, "I feel sorry for him. I don't really love him as I did before, but I do as a brother. I have a boyfriend now, and we are serious about each other. I have not had sexual relations with Ron for more than a year. That is why he is so depressed and upset. There are times when he actually becomes violent, almost crazed, and that frightens me. He was terribly angry when I refused to have sex with him the last time he approached me. I tried to tell him it was wrong and we shouldn't be doing it. Besides, I had a boyfriend. Ron was so angry he started to slam things around the house and threatened to kill me if I ever left him. It was too much. I was so glad to go to school just to be away from him. I feel better now that he is in the hospital, but I am worried that he will do something to hurt my boyfriend or me when he gets out."

This was a serious situation. The previous year, a Tulpehocken High School student had killed his former girlfriend with a shotgun, because she broke off their relationship after she recognized he was disturbed. I tried to comfort Tess. I told her that Ron would be on antidepressant medication, which would help. He still would need to be observed carefully for any signs of potential anger. What I said did not fully allay her fears. She left the office concerned for her safety and that of her boyfriend. The hospital physicians recognized they were dealing with a serious mental problem and that Ron was potentially very dangerous. He remained in the hospital for two and a half years and was only released after his father died.

In the meantime, Tess graduated from high school, married, and left the Bernville area with her new husband. She was afraid to make any local contact, and I never heard from her again. Ron did return home. I saw him on one or two occasions after his discharge from the State Hospital. The farm had deteriorated to the point that they no longer had animals or any workable equipment. The last I heard, he and his mother sold the farm and moved away. I never learned where they went or what happened to them. I wondered how Tess faired with all the sexual and emotional trauma that she experienced in that terrible relationship.

Not all incest cases end so tragically, but I am not aware of any that had a good result for any of the family members involved.

Treatments for psychosexual disorders are still painfully limited. Thankfully, victims are encouraged to seek help with openness and without shame. It took great bravery on the part of those children more than fifty years ago to speak up about the horrors their abusers were hiding.

CHAPTER 12

Upheavals, Loss and Transitions

The 1960s were a mess. Anyone who was an adult during that time recalls all of the crises we faced from year to year. The Vietnam War continued all through the sixties and into the seventies, presidents would come and go, but the war went on. We saw the rise of the women's movement, the youth movement, political scandals, and great economic hardships. The long lines at the gas pump, vicious fights that broke out over gas, the general increases in prices for energy are all too vivid in our memories. Several of my patients faced the terrible tragedy of losing a son in the war, while others struggled to help rehabilitate a returning son with injuries, both physical and emotional. Medicine was in turmoil and drug addiction was on the rise. In the face of all these changes and uncertainties, life went on, moving forward much as combat soldiers slogging along a muddy road to the front lines and an uncertain future.

At the end of office hours one day in the late fall of 1967, I was poring over the day's charts, adding notes and comments. I had begun to wonder more and more about the future of medical care. In the ten years since I had started, regulations had increased, the cost of malpractice insurance was slowly rising, hospitals were taking a larger role in the practice of medicine, more doctors were moving their offices into the hospital, and the insurance companies were slowly getting a tighter and tighter grip on the practice of medicine. Many barriers were beginning to appear between the patient and the doctor. Money seemed to motivate all of it. I began to think there was a good chance the practice of medicine was not going to get any better.

The seventies were crucial years for our country, and they marked some great changes in my life and that of my family. The local prison warden, Walter Scheipe, set off a series of events that triggered a domino effect. The warden called to see if I would be interested in being the consultant physician to Berks County Prison. I drove down to see him for a discussion of what the position would require in terms of my time and duties. The conversation went well. We formed an understanding and working relationship. I told him I would be interested in the position and could start anytime. My relationship with Warden Scheipe grew into a lifelong friendship.

My life had taken on several dimensions. No longer was I just a practicing country physician. I was operating a drug clinic and serving as the county prison physician and school physician for three school districts. I was doing research under a federal grant. I had developed several businesses including a reference laboratory for hospitals and a clinical laboratory for physicians, a manufacturing business for dairy hygiene, and a testing business for proof of efficacy for cosmetic products. Though I continued to see patients, I knew I was approaching another crossroad.

I was pulled in many directions, all of which required new knowledge, time and effort, as well as commitments. I had a hard time sorting out duty and obligation from interest and dedication. Although it was no longer my greatest interest, my practice always came first. I maintained regular office hours, but I no longer admitted patients to the hospital or delivered babies. I reduced my office hours to three afternoons a week and eliminated evening hours altogether in order to spend more time with my family. I still made emergency housecalls and had emergency hours on Saturdays.

During the seventies, there were more and more drug addicts in the prison population. I talked with the warden about starting a treatment program. Walter was receptive to the idea, but the question was, what kind of treatment program? No prison in Pennsylvania had a treatment program for drug addicts. I learned from a colleague that the University of Pennsylvania was experimenting with a methadone program. I met with the psychiatrist in charge of the program and was impressed. I was ready to consider this treatment the answer to our addiction problem at Berks County Prison. I started by prescribing methadone tablets for prisoners arriving heavily addicted to heroin, to help them through the withdrawal process. Within a week, I had dozens of heroin addicts from all over the county wanting to come to the office for treatment. I had no experience with drug addicts. I gave them prescriptions for methadone and tried to put them on a drug reduction program. It was a disaster. They were con artists. They used the prescription, selling the tablets and getting high. I could not control this abuse. I would need funds and a controlled facility with a staff to manage such a program. I had a visit from the DEA, demanding that I cease-and-desist dispensing methadone, because it was illegal. I was up to my ears in heroin addicts inside and outside the prison. I did not know what to do. Because of a legal snafu, I was now faced with a roadblock that could undermine my goal: to save the lives of people suffering in the grip of their addiction.

I was facing a crisis. There were more addicts than I could handle alone, and now I discovered I was violating federal law. As always, when I was facing an insurmountable obstacle, I prayed for help that something could be done.

A few days later, I received a call from the administrator of Community General Hospital in Reading. He offered me facilities at the hospital and a support staff of nurses to set up a drug treatment clinic. All I needed was the funds. The methadone clinic in Philadelphia had been approved by the state for drug treatment. My starting point was to duplicate that facility and to apply for state and federal funds. I did receive approval from the State of Pennsylvania to operate the clinic, but there were still no funds. The physician working in Philadelphia suggested I look at available federal funds and gave me the name of a contact who could help. In three weeks' time, I had federal funds for the methadone clinic, and we were on our way. We were one of only three clinics in the State approved for methadone treatment of heroin addicts.

I was thrown into an entirely new world, the murky, treacherous, and hazardous world of drug addicts. For the next six years, I experienced things that I could never have imagined nor dreamed of. I was deeply, but sadly, impacted by the addicts' disregard for life. Most drug users were aware that shooting heroin into their veins was a potentially lethal action. When I discussed this with them, they did not seem concerned. All they wanted was "the hit," the immediate rush, an escape from reality. The community of addicts who knew each other well held no loyalty or remorse for anyone who died of a "hotshot," an exceptionally potent dose. I was shocked to know their street friends' first question on hearing of a death was "Where's the bag?" meaning whether there was anything left of their drug stash. These people lived on the pleasure principle, regardless of the cost.

My eyes were opened to the ugly side of society, the indifference of the citizens toward the addicts, the corrupt law enforcement officers at the city, county, state and federal levels, good guys and the bad guys, and even a glimpse into the dark soul of the drug addict.

I met Curtis Jefferson, the biggest heroin dealer in the county, in the prison. He was a militant African-American male. I was warned by the prison staff that he was dangerous. He came into the infirmary requesting pills to help him sleep, known in the drug culture as Red Devils. I gave him three Seconal™ capsules. The next morning during regular infirmary hours, Curtis showed up and returned the pills. He told me that he really didn't need the capsules. He had been testing to see if I was humane enough to give him some consideration. I told him I was there to help the prisoners. We sat and talked for a while. He told me he was going to be getting out on bail that afternoon and expressed interest in coming to the methadone clinic to talk to me.

The next morning, the sheriff was gunning to return him to prison on a perjury charge. Curtis was returned to prison with bail set at $40,000. This trumped-up charge upset me.

I spoke to Judge Hess to try to arrange his release, but the judge could not release Curtis. I offered to put up bail personally. I did not want my gesture to be made public. The story was leaked anyway and made a considerable splash in the local paper. Curtis was released later that morning. He called me to set up an appointment to meet in a small restaurant on the outskirts of the city.

He wanted to know why I bailed him out.

"Curtis, I was outraged by the injustice."

Before I could say anything else, he told me that forty of the individuals in the methadone clinic were not addicts at all. They were just obtaining methadone to sell it. He had prepared a list of names for me. He gave me names of all of the city and state officials who were on his payroll. He explained that he could no longer deal drugs, because of his arrest. Curtis was not a drug user. In fact, most high-level drug dealers did not use drugs. Though he made a good deal of money in drug traffic, he was tired of the hassle and the risks and wanted to get out of it. His wife Sherry was encouraging him to stop dealing and to find something less risky to earn a living. Curtis stayed in the county until his trial. Since there was not enough evidence to convict him, he was set free.

He came to the clinic at Community General Hospital to thank me for what I had done for him. He had made a decision to be a minister. He was going to Philadelphia to study for the ministry. He laughed when he saw my surprise. I was genuinely happy for him and bid him good-bye.

Unfortunately, his life ended quickly and tragically. Curtis was found brutally beaten, dead on a city street. To this day, his murder remains unsolved.

Fred Stubbs was not a prisoner. His heroin addiction began while he worked third shift at one of Reading's largest factories, Dana Corporation. He was handsome and intelligent, with a radiant, infectious smile. Fred was known to all his friends as "Shug," for Sugar. When he entered the clinic, we had just started to use liquid methadone in orange juice. Each of the addicts drank the cocktail for their daily dose at the clinic. We had each addict say a few words to make sure he had swallowed the liquid. All the patients in the clinic received weekly urine tests for the presence of other drugs. New patients were screened for the presence of drugs to keep non-addicted people from obtaining methadone. We also checked their backgrounds thoroughly to make sure they were known addicts. In the end, I had to conclude that methadone is not an effective method of treatment, for we were able to rehabilitate only four addicts out of 150. More died from drug-related causes than we were able to save. Fred Stubbs was one of the very few addicts who had a successful recovery and went on to make major contributions to the city and county.

Our treatment program reduced the dosage of methadone until the patient was just taking orange juice. We would maintain the addict on plain orange juice for an additional eight weeks, without telling them they were completely clean. At the end of that period, we would reveal they were free of heroin and had been for the last two months! On Fred's day of discovery, his wild happiness brought the staff to tears. He jumped for joy, hands raised, clear through the ceiling tile. The imprint of his fingertips in that room remains there to this day. That afternoon, he began to look for a college to attend. Two years later, he graduated with an associate's degree from Reading Area Community College as the top member of his class. He went on to get a bachelor's degree in mental health at Alvernia College in Reading. Fred became the county mental health officer. He later retired from that position and started a center for domestic violence with his own money. Over three hundred families received counseling and help through Fred's work. He died of natural causes at the age of seventy, having left a greater legacy of accomplishment and community service than many I have known who had far more promising beginnings.

We discontinued the methadone program in the prison, because there were too many cases of prisoner abuses. Two prisoners had died. Eliminating all illegal drugs from the prison was near to impossible. We were forced to conclude that the addition of another potent drug only exacerbated the problem.

Our family was moving along life's path. Steve graduated from Georgetown Prep School and entered Franklin and Marshall College. Patti was starting high school, and Susan and Peter were working their way through grade school. I was deeply involved with my work with prisoners and drug addicts, but I was concerned about the proximity of my children. I frequently brought some of the addicts home with me after meetings. Though Joanne received them graciously, she confessed that she was afraid of them.

We hired an addict from the program as a live-in cook and housekeeper, in order to help her with her rehabilitation. It was a disaster. Bertha was an excellent cook, a skilled seamstress, and possessed a real talent in knitting, but her good qualities did not compensate for the fact that she was a prostitute. She lived in an apartment on the third floor of our home. At nighttime, she changed out of her white uniform and donned an "Afro" wig and "hot pants"—her street clothes. She would say goodnight, and her pimp would be waiting for her to deliver her to the streets of Reading. She returned with the dawn to assume her domestic duties. Joanne was horrified.

We were in the process of deciding what to do about Bertha, when a weekend guest mentioned that twenty dollars was missing from her purse. Even though she denied it vigorously, we knew that Bertha had stolen that money. We notified the prison, and she was returned that day. Having given her every consideration possible, we were not able to change her ways. Once she got out of prison, she continued to ply her trade for some years to come. Most of the prostitutes that I knew in prison and at the drug clinic met an early end. Some were beaten to death by their pimps. Others developed pelvic inflammatory disease or cervical cancer. The oldest survival age of any of these women I knew was thirty-seven.

My receptionist informed me the caller on the phone was Mr. Weaver. I knew several Mr. Weavers. Pappy Weaver, a ninety-year old, vigorous, irascible patriarch was on the phone. He called to complain that his daughter, Ruth, was unwilling to repair the barn roof. Ruth was a maiden lady in her mid-sixties, known to experience episodes of heart failure secondary to valvular heart disease. Ruth was about five feet six inches tall, quite muscular for a woman, and a bit overweight. She wore her hair combed straight back, covered with a little white cap as is the custom with Mennonite ladies. She dressed in dark Mennonite attire. Her face was suntanned as were her hands. Ruth always wore a smile on her face and was an absolute optimist. I explained to Mr. Weaver that it would be impossible for his daughter to re-shingle a ninety-foot barn roof. My explanation did not have much effect. I told him I would see his daughter and examine her. Grudgingly, he said he would make an appointment for her.

When I saw Ruth, her condition had grown markedly worse. She was in congestive heart failure, barely able to walk without severe respiratory distress. Her legs were swollen to the knees, a typical symptom of congestive heart failure. She had fluid in her chest, also an ominous sign associated with a failing heart. For the first time, Ruth really looked sick. The happy expression on her face was gone, though she tried to smile as we discussed her condition. Her color was pale and had a gray tone. All these symptoms suggested that her heart was in the last stages of complete failure. Her heart had compensated as much as it could over the years, but now the weak heart muscles could no longer keep up with her activity.

After the examination, I asked her how she felt. She answered in a weak voice between gasps for breath, "I don't feel well at all, Doctor. I am so tired all the time. I can't sleep, and I can just barely walk across a room. I cannot lie down without being very short of breath, and I cannot walk upstairs."

I told her she needed to see a cardiologist to be managed properly. She probably needed valvular heart surgery. We set up an appointment for the next day with the cardiology group. After examining her, the cardiologist agreed that she needed heart surgery, as she had reached the end of medical management. They felt the bilateral valve replacement was necessary. The operation had never been performed on anyone in the Berks County area. Ruth was referred to the cardiac surgical group at the University of Pennsylvania in Philadelphia.

Ruth responded extremely well to her historic surgery. She returned to the Reading cardiology group. Later, I saw her in my office. She was walking quite well, smiling and happy, and was in good shape.

"How are you feeling, Ruth?" I asked, as I approached her for the examination.

She replied in a strong confident voice and with her usual pleasant smile, "I'm a lot better than the last time I was here, Doctor. Thank you."

I explained that she could do mild housework, but that her days working on the farm were over—no more plowing, tractor driving, or repairing barns. Her sister, Darlene, who was a few years younger than Ruth, and in excellent physical condition, was with her. Darlene was a matter-of-fact lady, who always dressed in a lighter colored clothing than Ruth. Though she was always polite, she smiled only occasionally, being a very serious person. There was a quality about Darlene that made everyone feel comfortable in her presence, but I had the sense that there was much more to her than she would ever reveal. Darlene spoke up in response to my outlined activities for Ruth.

"I can assure you, Doctor, that Ruth will not be involved in any strenuous activity. When she is fully recovered, the only thing we will let her do is light housework." I noticed Ruth forming a smile on her lips. I didn't know whether it was a smile of relief and happiness at not having to work on the farm, or whether she figured that she was going to get involved in activities other than what I had outlined.

I saw Ruth once or twice again, and she continued to do well. She was a triumph of the new surgical specialty and treatment of cardiovascular disease at the University of Pennsylvania. It wasn't until 1970 that Berks County saw the first double valve transplant.

###

Not every situation ran smoothly in my practice. What happened with Lillie Elm is a case in point. She appeared in my office with hemorrhoids, for which I referred her to a rectal specialist. Something about her made me feel uneasy. I felt suspicious. I never had a good feeling in her presence. One day, she called our office from a pay phone. Her car had broken down, and she was unable to get a local garage to service her. The receptionist inquired why this was so, and Lillie gave her a hard time. When the receptionist consulted with me, I told her we were not in the taxi business and that Lillie should call a relative to help her. On receiving my message, she slammed down the receiver. We did not hear from her for a few days. One of my nurses, adept at ferreting out information, found out none of the local merchants would provide service to Lillie. She had cheated everyone and filed lawsuits against many of the merchants. I wondered more about this woman. She did not work, and her husband Leo was a laborer, yet they lived in an expensive new home.

The town grapevine revealed that Lillie had won a considerable award from a car dealer, for an injury she supposedly suffered at the dealership. She had three such awards in a period of two years. She had sprinkled the contents of a small bottle of water on the floor of a dealership while no one was looking. Then she fell down and started screaming. The dealer, to avoid notoriety, settled out of court. This is how Lillie earned her living. As I was leaving the office for the hospital one day, Lillie stopped me in the parking lot. She wanted me to sign a certificate for her husband, stating that he had been ill and had missed two weeks of work. I had not seen him in the office. In fact, I had driven by his house as he was working on a project outside. I refused to sign the paper.

Lillie was a short, overweight woman with small eyes and pouting lips. Her voice could be modulated to sound like a coy young girl or a seasoned Marine drill sergeant. When she was angry, she glared at you as she spoke. She wore her dyed black hair in a severe bobbed cut. She always seemed to wear loud, ill-fitting flowered dresses. Her feet and hands were disproportionately large for her height.

When I returned to the office from making rounds at the hospital, the secretary informed me that Lillie had been there. Lillie had given my secretary the sick certificate, explaining that she had just spoken to me in the parking lot and that I authorized the slip.

I was absolutely furious. First, I called her husband's place of work and explained to the nurse on duty that the sick certificate had been obtained falsely. I would not honor it. She informed me that it was not possible to do anything about it, because it would require an investigation by the union. The company did not want anything like that to happen, because of the complex nature of labor relationships. Knowing that Lillie was fully aware of this situation made me even angrier.

I discharged Lillie as a patient. I sent her a certified letter to that effect. Two days later, she appeared in my office with her daughter, Julia. Julia was a loud-mouthed, sixteen-year old. She was overweight like her mother. She wore a short skirt over fishnet stockings and too much makeup for a teenager. She spoke for Lillie, "My mother is having some sort of an attack."

Lillie was shaking and going through a ridiculous gyration, throwing her head backward, grunting and jerking her arms spastically. Any trained physician would immediately recognize this was a ruse. I let her daughter know I was not impressed.

"Your mother is not a patient," I said firmly. "I discharged her legally and officially, two days ago. I will not treat her, and she must leave my office immediately, or I will call the police."

"But my mother is sick! She needs help. You must treat her!" she pleaded, dramatically.

"There is absolutely nothing wrong with your mother. She is getting out of my office right now!" I demanded.

I took Lillie by the arm and informed her I was going to escort her out of the office and into her car. I would not allow her to fall down in my office and have cause to sue me. As soon as I got hold of her arm, she was miraculously cured and began to put up a fight. Twisting her arm, she tried to pull away from me. I held her arm firmly and ushered her down the steps, out of the office, and into her car. All the time she was screaming and cursing me. I told her that if I ever saw her on my property, I would have her arrested. That was the last I heard of her for a while. As they drove off, she swore at me, threatened me, gesturing wildly and shouting all sorts of vulgarities.

Several years passed before I received a call from Julia Elm concerning medical attention for her mother. She caught me at a time of day when I picked up my own phone. She immediately started to curse.

"Now, you son of a bitch, get your ass over here and take care of my mother, or I will have the law on you."

I explained curtly that I had no legal or professional obligation to see her mother.

She demanded again that I come to see her mother, again threatening me with legal action.

"Julia, you are wasting my time. I have no obligation to see any member of your family." I hung up on her.

A few moments later, the County Medical Society administrator called, wanting to know why I would not see this patient.

"Woody, I would be happy to answer you, but first, I would like you to call at least three of the following physicians: Dr. Yoh, Dr. Imber, Dr. Nagel, or Dr. Good, and ask them what they think about Lillie."

When he called back, he was amazed that I had treated her as long as I had. Each physician he called swore as soon as he heard the name. That was enough for him. I never heard from her again, although an innocent patient of mine would later fall victim to the curse of Lillian, quite literally.

The Pennsylvania Dutch people, for many hundreds of years, have believed in a type of witchcraft known as hexing. They believe that some people have "powwow," the power to use hexing to cure disease. Other individuals can place a curse, or hex, on a person. These individuals are called *hexerie*. A patient appeared in my office one day, complaining of intractable diarrhea. Her name was Margaret. She was a woman in her fifties, thin and worn-looking. Her sun-damaged face was not unattractive, and she retained some semblance of a female figure. She was wearing a plain black dress, with a belt, and simple flat shoes. She wore her hair in a black bun streaked with gray.

Her family had lived in the Tulpehocken area for hundreds of years. Prosperous farmers and merchants, they owned several farms. They originally were French Huguenots, who later intermarried with the German settlers, including some of the Hessian troops that remained here after the Revolutionary War. While taking Margaret's history, I learned she had seen several doctors over the years, including two gastroenterologists. Since she was a woman of means, I referred her directly to the University of Pennsylvania for a comprehensive workup to find a cause for the diarrhea. While she was in Philadelphia, she appeared to be perfectly fine. Considering this, I came to the conclusion that what she had was a conversion reaction.

Margaret's case represented a mind-over-matter phenomenon. There is so much evidence that the mind has a powerful influence over the body, both positively and negatively. Feats of great strength, remarkable endurance, and uncanny perception all have been documented. On the other hand, many people have died as a result of their own minds. One of the many psychological mechanisms available to us as humans is the phenomena known as conversion. This process involves mental energy, produced by some internal distress that is converted to a physical energy that affects one part of the body. The most common areas afflicted are the brain, manifested by headaches, the skin with ill-defined "rashes," and the gastrointestinal system, with simple indigestion, ulcers, or diarrhea. We know so little about the mind and its powers over the body. It remains a vast field for medical research.

I explained to Margaret that this condition was triggered by her nerves and that she would have to see a nerve specialist. Actually, I was referring her to a psychiatrist. Dr. John Bower, an old-time Pennsylvania Dutch physician, was well-schooled in Dutch lore. After he saw my patient, he called me to discuss her situation.

"Puggy, this is a classic case of hexing. This woman has hexing bred into her bones. She is absolutely convinced that her neighbor is hexing her. She will drive fifteen miles out of her way to avoid passing in front of her neighbor's house. There is nothing that you can do. The only advice you can give her is to stay away from this woman."

"Should I then tell her that she is hexed?" I asked.

"Yes, absolutely. She already firmly believes that she is hexed. Not only will you gain credibility with her, Pete, but you will establish the basis of an ongoing therapy. On the other hand, if you ignore it, or deny it, you will not only lose her confidence, but she will get progressively worse." His response was definitive.

I had to ask, "Did she tell you the name of the woman who was hexing her?"

"Oh yes," he answered, "her name is Lillie."

A light dawned. My patient lived only three houses away from Lillie Elm on the same road!

When Margaret came into the office, I explained her condition in terms of Pennsylvania Dutch lore. She sat across from me in my consultation room, sitting on the very edge of her chair. The anxious expression on her face was intermingled with a high degree of fear and hope.

"Do you know what the problem is now, Doctor?" she asked softly, visibly concerned.

"Yes, Margaret, and I suspect you know it too. You are hexed. The only way you can be free of this curse is to avoid any contact with the hexing person," I explained.

Then she asked me, "Is it possible that a powwow doctor could help to break the spell?"

"I am not aware of anyone who could help you. Dr. Bower has a lot of experience with this type of condition and understands hexing very well. The only thing that you can do is to avoid being near her. Then you will be okay." To further reassure her that I was equipped to make this recommendation, I informed her that an elderly Dutch woman close to the family had told me this, years before.

For the first time since I had seen her, a thin smile crossed her lips and her eyes widened slightly. With the stress drained from her face, I could see that she had been a pretty woman. I told her she was welcome, any time, to call me, but that I felt her problem was now solved. She left the office standing straighter and with a lighter step. She had spent thousands of dollars just to prove what she already suspected.

Margaret lived out the rest of her life productively, happily gardening, and free of the fear of her hexing neighbor. I remember seeing her in the summer and fall, sitting on the side of the road with a small produce stand, greeting people, and selling her vegetables.

Life lessons fall into one of three categories. Some are useful, some are not only useless but even harmful, and some can be life-saving. One bitter cold night, I experienced an automatic recall of a special skill I had learned in the Marines two decades earlier that got me out of a tough situation in one piece.

Barbed Wire Holmes was one of the rarest men I have ever met. A master sergeant, Holmes was a no-nonsense, dedicated career Marine who went strictly by the book. He earned the name Barbed Wire Holmes during World War I, because he used his backpack as a buffer while throwing himself over coiled strands of barbed wire found abundantly in the Western Front trench warfare. The remaining Marines in his squad ran across his back to clear the barbed wire unharmed. His technique was adopted by many Marine companies during World War I.

I met Holmes in 1946, while he was having a beer with a few old comrades stationed in the area. One of his buddies that night was a platoon sergeant from my company. Sergeant Bacon called me over to the table, invited me to sit with them, and introduced me to Holmes and the other noncoms there. I remember being honored by this gesture, for this was a very exclusive group. With less than a year in the Marine Corps, I was a boot if ever there was one, just out of "boot camp." Sergeant Bacon had introduced me to the group at the table as "a very smart guy who doesn't belong in the Marine Corps." They all laughed at that and gave me a beer. I sat down and listened to their tales of combat, the days of the Death March on Corregidor, and their memories of miserable officers. More than sixty years later, the memory of that night is still fresh and exciting.

About a week later, I sat next to Holmes during lunch in the mess hall. We got on the topic of hand-to-hand combat. I asked him why the Marine Corps did not teach it in basic training beyond bayonet training. He told me something that I did not fully appreciate then, but never forgot. He looked at me straight in the eye and emphasized his points by tapping a finger on the table.

"Hand-to-hand combat is really hand-to-hand killing. If you can't kill the enemy with your rifle or your bayonet, then you're not going to have much luck in hand-to-hand combat," he said. "That is okay for the movies and storybooks, but in the real world of combat, your main purpose is to kill. All the fancy things that you learn in judo are of no value if they do not end up killing the enemy."

"I always wanted to learn hand-to-hand combat," I replied.

"Why?" Holmes asked me. "You are not a combat Marine and never will be. If you stay in here, you will end up either as an officer or in some administrative noncoms job."

"I want to know how to protect myself if I should ever need to," I explained.

He looked me over, as though he was evaluating a used car or a horse or anything that he was going to buy and invest time and money in. All that mattered to Sergeant Holmes was what I was made of and what he could do with me.

"If you want to learn self-defense, I can't help you. I am a paid killer. I am trained to kill. I do not fight. I kill. I can teach you to kill, but that is all I can teach you." He stopped speaking, leaned back, and waited for my answer. If I had hesitated, I would probably never have seen him again. I studied his weathered, steely face and said, "I want to learn to kill."

I knew I had said those words, but I could not believe my own ears. I did not want to kill anybody. I was preparing to study medicine so I could save lives. He knew that. But I felt there was a lot to learn from Sergeant Holmes, and I did not want to lose the opportunity. The experience would be painful, and I was not sure that what I learned would ever be helpful. Nonetheless, we made plans to meet that evening after chow at a designated exercise field. I had no idea what I had just gotten myself into.

Holmes was a dedicated instructor, relentless and demanding. The five-day conditioning he put me through was excruciating. I did not know a human being could survive that kind of abuse, but somehow I did. Each night after our training, we would go to the service club. Over a few beers, he explained what he was teaching me. He repeatedly reminded me that this skill was to be used only to kill an opponent. Those words were drummed into me every day with every technique that he taught me.

The next month of training was the most physically demanding period of my life. Several times, I wanted to give up the whole thing, but I could not give up, even if it killed me, which at one point during my training I was sure would happen. There were days when every bone in my body cried out in pain. Sometimes I was so fatigued I feared I would never move. I had bruises I thought would never heal.

I survived those thirty days. It changed my whole attitude about combat training and the meaning of the specially trained troops. The last thing that Sergeant Holmes said to me before we parted was, "Puggy, what you have learned, you have learned well. Don't think for a minute you know everything. There are plenty of guys who know more than you, who have a lot more skill than you. Remember just one thing. If you ever need to use what you have learned, you are trained to kill. Do not hesitate."

Those words were frightening. I had acquired a deadly skill that I had to control. He went on to say, "Never forget that the enemy you are engaging is an evil son-of-a-bitch and will show you no mercy. He is out to kill you!" I didn't intend to forget, but I did not suspect that Barbed Wire Holmes' words would ever become a reality.

The ringing phone shattered the quiet of one evening with a shrill call to duty. A teenage girl, Pauline Willow, was on the line. A picture of her came to mind. She was homely and slovenly. Her hair was matted, a dingy blonde. Her deeply sunken eyes were small and hidden under bushy eyebrows. Her teeth were crooked and decaying. During the call, Pauline complained of abdominal pain and nausea. I asked if she had a fever. She replied that she didn't have a thermometer, but she didn't feel warm.

I decided it would be best to see this girl, because abdominal pain can present a serious diagnostic challenge at times. She no longer lived with her mother. Though I did not recognize the place she described, I knew the general area and could find it. I hugged my understanding wife good-bye. "Joanne, I will be gone at least two hours. You can reach me on the car phone if you need me." Decades before cell phones, I had installed a portable telephone in my car, since not all homes I visited had telephone service. The equipment was enormous. The transponder filled the trunk of my Lincoln Continental. On many occasions, that advanced communications technology helped save the day as I traveled on those unmarked country roads.

The house was located in a wooded area several miles from Shartlesville. When I drove through the woods to the house, I saw only one light burning in an upper story room. The dilapidated clapboard house was dark and weathered.

A light appeared at the doorway when I pulled into the yard. A young man came to greet me. "She's upstairs," he said. He was a tall, thin teenager not more than nineteen years old, with sharp facial features, a straggly beard, and a ponytail secured with a wide green rubber band. He wore jeans, a beat-up brown leather jacket, and a stocking cap.

I walked up the dimly lit stairs, followed by the young man, and entered into a dark bedroom. There were two other teenage boys in the room. Pauline had a reputation in the community as a very promiscuous girl. The first time I saw her in the office she was fifteen. Not only did she have the worst case of crab lice I had ever seen, but she also had a venereal infection. When questioned about the partner who may have given her this infection, she laughed and said, "Partner? I have had sex with so many guys, I would never know who gave it to me!"

I did feel uneasy about the presence of three males in her bedroom. I wondered what was going on. It felt like a setup. As a precaution, I walked to the other side of the bed, putting the bed between me and the three young men who were standing together against the far wall. I appraised the three individually, because I felt it was only a matter of time before they attacked me. I placed my medical bag near the wall, out of reach from the guys in the room. The atmosphere was ominous. This housecall was obviously not for a medical emergency.

The first boy, who greeted me, was the shiftiest-looking one of the group, but physically, I did not think he would be a problem. He had the appearance and posture of a coward. The boy in the middle was a different story. He was about 5'8" with a crew cut, possibly an ex-military man. He was muscular, with a short, strong neck. I estimated he was probably twenty years old. He would clearly present the greatest problem. In the event of an attack, I would have to take him on first. The third boy was small. He seemed to be older, most likely in his early twenties. He had bucked teeth and a nervous twitch of his head. He was wearing a baseball cap, backward, and an ill-fitting turtleneck sweater. I noticed a small baseball bat in his right hand. He had separated himself quite a few feet from the other two boys. I could not read the significance of that position. As I proceeded toward the bed to examine Pauline, two of the boys moved away from the wall, approaching the foot of the bed.

I greeted Pauline. "Hello, Pauline, are you still having pain?"

"Yes, Doctor. I can still feel it, here," she replied to my question.

"How long have you had it?" I asked, moving closer to the bedside.

"Well, I think it started this morning, but it seems to come off and on."

I asked her if she would pull down the cover, so I could examine her abdomen. I questioned her further about any urinary or bowel symptoms, which might suggest a urinary tract infection. She complied. The soiled blanket was thrown to one side, revealing that she was wearing a pair of tight slacks and a blouse.

Pauline lay on the dirty bed, her hands on her chest, her head turned toward me. She did not look one bit ill.

I took off my gloves, my hat, my scarf, and overcoat and placed them on a rickety wooden chair next to the bed. Joanne had often warned me never to put my coat on a bed, because of the possibility of bed bugs. I rubbed my hands to warm them, as I asked her what other signs and symptoms she had and whether she was having her period or if she was constipated.

She answered "No." She had no vomiting. She had not eaten since noon time, but said she'd had a Coke about an hour earlier. I took her hand to check her pulse and then proceeded to examine her abdomen. There was no sign of any pathological process taking place other than the fact that she needed a bath. All this time, the three boys looked at me intensely, shifting their positions, moving back and forth, in a restless motion that was building up to something.

When I determined that she was not having any serious abdominal problem, I let her know that she was okay. Whatever had been wrong with her was not serious, I assured her, and that she would not need any medication or further treatment. She looked at me with an expression that telegraphed, "Don't you get what's going on here?" It was not an expression of concern for my welfare. She seemed proud to have gotten me there.

She pulled up the blanket and glanced over at the three teenagers, all now standing against the wall. That look was clearly a signal.

As I turned to retrieve my overcoat and scarf, the three boys mobilized their aggression, moving toward me. They obviously planned to mug me and to steal whatever money and drugs I had with me. I took stock of my opponents. The boy nearest to me was the tall, thin one. The third, smaller, boy looked frightened. The club in his hand was slightly raised. There was no mistaking their intention.

Almost instantly, everything I had learned twenty years earlier from Sergeant Holmes surfaced and transformed me. The boys had made their way to the bottom of the bed. I looked the muscular one, obviously the leader, squarely in the eyes. I said, forcefully, "Stop! Don't move!"

They hesitated.

"I am a Marine trained not to fight but to kill. If you get anywhere near me, one of you will die, and one of you will be maimed and crippled for life. The third one doesn't matter, because I can do anything to him I want to do. Whoever comes at me first is a dead man."

Looking at each other, they shuffled hesitantly. For a moment, I thought they would all rush me at once. I had my hands raised in an offensive position, ready for anything. The one with a crew cut blurted out, "We're not going to hurt you. We just want your money and the drugs." Knowing that they were confused and uncertain, I pressed my advantage. They were beginning to lose their nerve. I said, "Back off and get against the far wall. I do not want to hurt you, but I will kill you if you come near me."

The smallest one moved away first, followed by the tall, thin boy. The muscular one took his time, glancing back at me. They moved to the corner of the room, mumbling that they were not going to hurt me, but I did not respond to them. I took my hat, coat, scarf, and gloves, picked up my bag, and walked out of the room to the stairwell. I stopped in the doorway, turned to the girl, and warned, "Pauline, don't you ever call me again."

They did not follow me.

Twenty years later, Sergeant Holmes' training had been tested. My mind and body had been deeply programmed. This primitive part of me feels not too far removed from the jungle. Recognizing this quality gives me insight into how difficult it is to control our base nature, even though our spiritual side pulls us toward God.

I wondered what would have happened if those boys had attacked me. It would have been a disaster. I would have acted entirely on instinct with one thought in mind—to destroy the enemy. This ability was as much a part of me as going to church, reading medical journals, or making hospital rounds. I knew if I told Joanne about this, she would worry tremendously. She was riddled with fears for my safety. I decided not to tell her about the threatening situation.

Joanne was still up and waiting for me, as she usually was when I returned from a late-night call. We had hot chocolate and a piece of buttered toast at the kitchen table and reviewed the day. She looked at me without smiling, clearly worried.

"What was wrong with the Willow girl?" she asked.

"Nothing serious, I think she just was ovulating and had a little *mittleschmerz*."

"Are you sure that was all?" she replied, doubting my response.

"Yes, why do you ask?"

"Peter, you have that look that something unpleasant happened, something you do not want to tell me about," she explained, her blue eyes focused on me.

There was nowhere to go but to tell her. "I didn't want to tell you, because I know you worry easily. But, yes. There was nothing wrong with her. There were three boys with her, and they planned to rob me, but I was able to talk them out of it."

Her porcelain skin flushed, furiously. "My God, Peter!" she exclaimed, "You could have been hurt, or even killed!"

"There was no danger, honey," I said, keeping my voice even, "I could easily have taken those three boys. I really wasn't worried for my safety."

"Well!" she said emphatically, "If that girl ever calls again, I am really going to give her a piece of my mind, in no uncertain terms!"

"I told her never to call again and that I would not see her as a patient. I think she was more frightened than the boys." We let it go at that. I was reminded that every time I went on a housecall, my Joanna worried until I returned.

Michael Spaeth was only a four-year-old child, but he was one of the most unusual and charming patients that ever graced my office. He was the firstborn of Jane and Samuel Spaeth, a young couple who lived with the husband's parents on a dairy farm. Many families had several generations living in the same home as part of the traditional way of life of the Pennsylvania Dutch. In fact, I recall as a young lad growing up in Reading that most of the families were multiple, that is, at least two, often three, generations were living in the same home.

Jane's pregnancy and delivery had been textbook perfect. Michael was born on a cold February morning at three o'clock in the Reading Hospital. I was struck by the amount of raven black hair and large blue eyes that greeted me on his entrance into the world. During his first year of life, I can recall that he was always a very pleasant baby, constantly smiling and very friendly. Michael walked at one year of age and was talking at two years. By the time he was three, he had acquired quite an extensive and sophisticated vocabulary. I remember well the time when he was three years old, I called him, "Mickey." He informed me quite seriously that his name was Michael, not Mickey. He was in every way a lovable and perfect child, but surely his own man.

The purpose of his visit today was his four-year checkup. He seemed a little indignant when I put him on the pediatric table, saying that he thought that table was just for babies. I explained that I used the table not only to weigh him but also to make it easier to examine him.

"All right, I understand." He flashed me a patient, knowing smile. During the examination, he had many questions about what I was doing, and why I used certain instruments. He was quite curious about the rubber percussion hammer that we used to check reflexes of nerves. He wanted to know why it was made of rubber, when all the hammers that he knew about were made of steel. I explained to him that the rubber hammer is not for driving nails but to test nerves and that it was easier on the patient and the doctor. He also expressed great interest in the stethoscope, wanting to know what I heard in his chest and what his heart sounded like.

After the examination, I exchanged a few pleasantries with his mother, inquiring about her little two-year-old daughter. Then, as was my custom with pediatric patients, I asked Michael if he would like a Tootsie Roll pop. I was surprised when he looked up at me and shook his head in a negative motion.

"You don't want a lollipop, Michael? Why?" I asked him.

He looked at me with those big blue eyes and held up his little closed left hand. He then pushed two fingers up and spread them in a small V-shape as he said to me, "I want these many . . . one for my little sister."

Joanne and I had arrived in Bernville as strangers, with almost no money, but with a great deal of love and lofty aspirations to make a success of our life here. But as much as we wanted for ourselves, perhaps more so, our goal was to offer a first-class medical service to the people of our community.

It has been almost forty years since I struggled with the decision to either stay in medicine as a country doctor or go into research to try to help discover the causes of disease. My heart was no longer in clinical medicine. Since many of my patients were in their seventies and afflicted with so-called aging diseases, I became increasingly interested in the root causes of aging. I made the decision to close my practice and to pursue my other passions. While not all of my patients were cooperative, my memory is that most of them were pleasant, thanking me for the times we spent together and wishing me well in my endeavors.

I decided that I would leave my practice at the end of March. Most of my patients, although unhappy with my leaving, seemed to understand why I chose this path. That is, everyone but Amanda Hottenstein, the same spirited gal who had fallen down the steps at her son's home years earlier. Amanda was well past ninety when I called her to let her know that I would no longer be her doctor and that a new doctor would take care of her. Her response came as a total surprise to me.

"Yes, well, Doctor, I'll call you when I need you."

"Amanda, I'm afraid you did not understand what I said. I will not be practicing medicine any longer," I replied.

Her voice came over the line with strength and a message that was very authoritative and very definitive.

"Don't talk so dumb! You are my doctor, and I will call you when I need you."

That was the end of the conversation, and she hung up. She was the only patient I continued to treat, and she still lived with her son Curtis, now a widower. We went through some terrible times, with several bouts of pneumonia, a large dorsal basal cell carcinoma, several serious falls, and a host of minor incidences. In all that time, Amanda never once missed having her hair done at home on Saturday morning. Every time I saw her, it was a housecall. Even the surgery to remove her skin cancer was done on the kitchen table with my youngest son, Peter, as my assistant. Shortly after I left practice, Curtis sold the farm and they built a beautiful home along Garfield Road. It was a one-story modern rancher with all of the modern-day conveniences. I drank many a cup of coffee in that comfortable kitchen, overlooking the green valley and rolling hills, enjoying Dutch cookies at Amanda's table with her and Curtis. Amanda lived to be 103 years old. She died of pneumonia peacefully in her bed, the very same bed she shared with her husband on their wedding night.

How wonderful it was to deliver babies, follow them as they grew up, watch the families prosper, and see young couples growing into mature citizens. I was also privileged to attend to them in their most intimate tragedies, to help them when they were dying, and help to support the relatives of the dying. It was only after my experience with Ernie that I was aware of the significance of death and how important the role of the physician can be with a dying patient. I owe my patients so much for the education that they gave me, for helping me to understand the Bernville community, and for their many generosities in the years that I practiced medicine.

One day, after a visit from one of our Bernville friends, Joanne and I were sitting on the patio, enjoying a beautiful fall evening. I turned to her and said, "You know what I'm thinking?"

"I never know what you're thinking." She laughed.

"I was thinking of that famous line by Winston Churchill during the war when he was speaking of the soldiers: 'Never have so many, owed so much, to so few.'"

It came to my mind when I thought of our friends in Bernville and of all the years we lived here and all of the many thoughtful and kind things we had experienced. These people remain in my prayers, and I owe a debt to all of them.

As we sat there, we talked about our children, how accomplished they had each become, the partners they had chosen. It was interesting how the children adjusted quickly to the Bernville culture, even picking up the Pennsylvania Dutch accent well enough so that all four of them could do a perfect imitation. Steven went to Georgetown Prep outside Washington, DC, for high school, and Peter went to the Hill School in Pottstown, Pennsylvania. Joanne was very reluctant to send the girls away to private school. She was afraid for them to be away from home and her influence. Patti and Susan therefore graduated from Tulpehocken High, successfully navigating their teen years with activities and friends in their hometown before heading off to college.

In the last three decades, I have become a recognized expert on skin care and the physiology of aging. I have written four instructional books on the science of skin care for professional practitioners. When Joanne first asked me if I could develop something for the tiny line on her face that she viewed as a harbinger of aging, I knew nothing about skin care, or cosmetics. To please her, I began to study skin physiology and cosmetic chemistry, and as a result, a whole new world opened before me. You never know where life will take you when you stay open to all chances and possibilities coming your way, however obscure a path may seem at the time.

Today, at eighty-eight years of age, after reflecting on my life, and remembering the people in these stories I have shared with you, I can say this with certainty: an obstacle is often a diversion to a more rewarding opportunity. Someone said that every great fortune is the result of either a great crime or a great disaster. Those of us who are in our senior years know this to be true. In our lifetime, Joanne and I faced many actual and potential disasters, but with the grace of God, we were able to withstand them and turn them into minor miracles.

As I write down these stories, it has now been thirty-six years since I saw my last patient and said good-bye to my staff. I cranked the key until it clicked in the heavy black lock of the clinic. I drove down the lane, home to my wonderful wife. It was a little earlier than I usually arrived, but I was ready to be home. I remember walking into the kitchen, greeting Joanne with a kiss, and saying, "Well, it's finally over. I saw my last patient."

"Good," she smiled. "Dinner's not quite ready, dear. How about a cookie?"

Afterword:
The Finger of God

The process of living is often described as a journey along the road. Without question, life is definitely a journey, but it is a journey with a definite goal. Looking back over my lifetime, I firmly believe that the goal of every human being is to return to God. Why do I say that? Surely there must be other reasons in life, other purposes, so why God? I know very few people who ever seriously ask what life is all about, never stopping to consider the three fundamental questions of existence: What are we? Who are we? Why are we? It is the search for the answers to these three questions that represents the sum total of my life. Every human has the innate intelligence to search for these answers and to find them.

If one observes carefully, one sees that we move through life not so much with the view of what lies ahead, but constantly looking over our shoulders at the past, the dark specter of doubt and regret haunting our existence. Fear is characteristic of human nature. Alone in the darkness of night, we fear the unknown beyond us. The ferocious Cave Bear that tormented our Stone Age ancestors has been substituted with looming catastrophic war or financial ruin or a lost love. The monster is still under the bed.

Within each of us, there is a child who never completely becomes an adult. It is the child in us that is afraid. A memory drifted into my mind one day, as they often do when I am occupied with something else. In this case, I was in my woodworking shop. I could see myself as a very small child, not yet three years old. I could see my paternal grandfather, Pietro, getting up from his chair at the kitchen table, turning to me, and saying, *Veni qua, Chicolone, facciamo due passi.* "Come, little butterball, let us take two steps." He would extend a strong forefinger, which I reached up to grasp with my chubby child's hand, and we would go for a walk. I had no concerns about where we were going, because I had no fear as I held my grandfather's finger. I felt both love and security in that work-worn finger, walking beside him, connected.

It was at the moment of reflection on that scene that I realized that the answer to our fears is to regain, and retain, that childlike faith of believing that we must look only to the parents for security and well-being. The message in the teachings of all faiths is the same. *God is Our Father.* He does love us, and we must have *faith* in him.

If we humans, as we grow into adults, could retain that faith in God as our parent, it would be all that we would need to reach our final goal, eternal happiness with God.

Yes, it seems so simple, but so are all of the most wonderful things of this life. God did not make the world so complex that we could not understand it, nor did he create us without giving us the intelligence to understand it. The answer to all my searching was this truth: God is our Father. Everything else emanates from this.

I have shared some of my own life pattern of obstacles and miracles through these stories. Everyone has experiences in life that are pivotal, and some are catastrophic. For most of us, the worst is the death of a loved one. After sixty-one years of marriage to my beautiful Joanne, I stood by her bed and watched her die. Less than one year into her miraculous recovery from a stroke, she began to show unexplained muscle weakness, stricken with amyotrophic lateral sclerosis, commonly called Lou Gehrig's disease. The day after her eighty-first birthday, we were at Hershey Medical Center when we heard the diagnosis of ALS, and we both cried, for we knew her life on earth, and our life together, was coming to a close.

The anguish and the pain of losing a lifetime companion, whether inch by inch or through a sudden death, can only be understood by those who have had the experience. Only belief in God and the afterlife is able to assuage the horrible torment of this loss. I know that Joanne lives on in an existence completely unknown to us, the survivors. I feel that she is with me though I cannot physically contact her. I know she's here.

In the process of writing this book, less than three years after Joanne's death, my son, Peter, died unexpectedly at the age of forty-nine. While I was prepared for many things, the loss of my youngest child was not one of them. Peter had been struggling with alcoholism for many years, but he, like many alcoholics, did not realize he had a serious problem that would affect his body adversely. He died of a massive internal hemorrhage secondary to cirrhosis of the liver. The stark realization that I would not be able to speak with him, nor be with him, nor help him, was crushing. Again, I turned to God for support. I could sense the hand of God extended to me. I had only to reach out and grasp it. It is so unbelievable to me now that so often in tragedy we turn our backs on God, when all He is trying to do is to love us.

While I long for my beloved Joanne and Peter, I know that they are together, with God, and happy. I know that I am not alone. My three children, Steven, Patti, and Susan, and their spouses, are extremely supportive, and I'm eternally thankful to God for having them near to me. My adult grandsons have rewarded me abundantly with the success of their lives—Michael built a global organization in professional skin care products and education. Steven became a doctor, now a pulmonary specialist who recently presented me with my first great-grandchild, Sam. My granddaughter Lauren is a budding journalist, while Garman navigates first grade at the newly renovated school that once held all the grades from kindergarten to senior year. I pray that Kiara and Ethan will know the loving heritage of their father. Through my children and their families, I know that the life Joanne and I envisioned when we arrived in Bernville, with two little kids and a pocketful of dreams, was worth everything that we went through. This farm is our family's home, and the call of the Green Peepers still welcomes the spring.

While this book has been a look backward to my days as a clinician, I want you to know that I am looking forward to new ventures and new experiences. Along with many other scientists, I believe that aging is not an inevitable consequence of living. I believe rather it is an inflammatory disease that robs us of vitality and incapacitates us, until it slowly extinguishes the flickering candlelight of life. This need not be! While *time* continues to be a mysterious quantity in the totality of life, we have a long way to go toward understanding the role and nature of time. Surely time and aging are linked in some manner.

Physiologically, man should live eight times his sexually mature age, as do most mammals. Humans do not mature sexually until they are at least twenty years old, though this news is not acceptable to teenagers, but it is nevertheless a fact. That means that the normal lifespan of a human should be 160 years. Only one individual has approached that, Jeanne Calment of France lived to be more than 122 years old and died in 1997. We have to add less than forty years to Madame Calment's age to reach that goal. This is not an impossible task, considering that in 1900, life expectancy was forty-seven years; now it is more than eighty years. The question becomes, what are we to do with these extra years? We could utilize them by employing our God-given intelligence to make the most of them. We definitely need to hold the finger of God along the way.

I want to leave the reader with this thought. You need not be afraid. God your Father is always with you. You just need to reach out to him. God will never force you to do anything. It is your love of God that makes you a good person and that gives you strength to bear the burdens of life and to survive the tragedies. There is nothing that could happen to you that is so bad that God could not help you. We cannot know the horrors that have happened to many people, nor why we are spared. Do not expect to understand all of the things that happened to you in life.

Whenever you have a loss of something important, whatever it may be, remember that God gave it to you in the beginning, and be thankful for that. I thank God for letting me share sixty-three years of my life with my beloved Joanne and for the life of our Peter. The joy of those years cannot be blotted out by the physical loss of my wife and son. God loves us, otherwise, we would not be.

Finally, God is love. All the philosophy of the world is summed up in those words.

It is my hope that within these stories of my patients, something may bring you a smile, a measure of comfort, or an insight that will help you to better understand yourself, a friend, or your fellow man. We are all in this life together. We have the gift of life, and it is a glorious gift.

Know that you are never alone. Just as my grandfather offered his finger to me to hold, making me feel so safe and loved, God the Father says to each of his children, "Come and walk with me." We have only to reach up and hold on.